Cambridge Latin Course

Cambridge Latin Course

Book V
FOURTH EDITION

CAMBRIDGE
UNIVERSITY PRESS

CAMBRIDGE
UNIVERSITY PRESS

University Printing House, Cambridge CB2 8BS, United Kingdom

Cambridge University Press is part of the University of Cambridge.

It furthers the University's mission by disseminating knowledge in the pursuit of education, learning and research at the highest international levels of excellence.

Information on this title: education.cambridge.org

© University of Cambridge School Classics Project 2003

First published 1971
7th printing 1982
Second edition 1986
13th printing 2002
Fourth edition 2003
15th printing 2016

Printed in Dubai by Oriental Press

A catalogue record for this publication is available from the British Library

ISBN 978-0-521-79792-4 Paperback

Front and back cover photographs: Roger Dalladay
Drawings by Peter Kesteven, Joy Mellor and Leslie Jones

ACKNOWLEDGEMENTS

Thanks are due to the following for supplying photographs, drawings and paintings for reproduction: p. 14, p. 17, p. 44, p. 62*b*, p. 96, Photo Scala, Florence; p. 28, Colchester Museums; pp. 38–9, p. 85, AKG London/Peter Connolly; p. 46 *b*, p. 62 *t*, p. 73 *l*, *r*, p. 97, © Copyright The British Museum; p. 64 *b*, © 1998 White Star S.r.l.; p. 83 *tr*, Yale University Press.

Other photography by Roger Dalladay.

Thanks are due to the following for permission to reproduce photographs: p. 7 *t*, *b*, Museo Boscoreale, Pompeii; p. 11 *t*, p. 20, p. 23, p. 29, p. 80 *t*, p. 98, Museo della Civiltà Romana; p. 11 *b*, Vill Adriana, Tivoli; p. 13, Villa of Piazza Armerina, Sicily; p. 30, Museo Archeologico Nazionale, Naples; p. 39, p. 48, p. 83 *bl*, *br*, p. 84, Soprintendenza of the Forum Romanum; p. 94, Soprintendenza, Pompeii.

Every effort has been made to reach copyright holders. The publishers would be glad to hear from anyone whose rights they have unknowingly infringed.

Contents

RUS

STAGE 35

ex urbe

When you have read this story, answer the questions on the next page.

Mānius Acīlius Glabriō salūtem dīcit Lupō amīcō.
quid agis, mī Lupe, in vīllā tuā rūsticā? quid agit Helvidius,
fīlius tuus?

    quotiēns dē tē tuāque vīllā cōgitō, tibi valdē invideō; nam in
urbe nusquam est ōtium, nusquam quiēs. ego quidem multīs   *5*
negōtiīs cotīdiē occupātus sum. prīmā hōrā ā clientibus meīs
salūtor; inde ad basilicam vel cūriam contendō; aliquandō
amīcōs vīsitō, vel ab eīs vīsitor; per tōtum diem officia prīvāta
vel pūblica agō. at tū intereā in rīpā flūminis vel in umbrā
arboris ōtiōsus fortasse iacēs, et dum ego strepitū urbis vexor, tū   *10*
carmine avium dēlectāris. sed satis querēlārum!

    Imperātor Domitiānus triumphum heri dē Germānīs ēgit.
pompa, per tōtam urbem prōgressa, ā multīs laudābātur, ā
nōnnūllīs dērīdēbātur. aliī 'spectāculum splendidissimum!'
clāmābant. 'Imperātor noster, pater vērus patriae, gentēs   *15*
barbarās iam superāvit; Germānī per viās urbis iam in triumphō
dūcuntur!' aliī tamen 'spectāculum rīdiculum!' susurrābant. 'illī
quī per viās dūcuntur haudquāquam Germānī sunt, sed servī, ex
prōvinciā Hispāniā arcessītī et vestīmenta Germāna gerentēs!'

    litterae cotīdiē ā Britanniā exspectantur, ubi Agricola bellum   *20*
contrā Calēdoniōs gerit. Calēdoniī crēduntur ferōcissimī
omnium Britannōrum esse. dē Calēdoniā ipsā omnīnō incertus
sum, mī Lupe. utrum pars est Britanniae an īnsula sēiūncta?

    ad cōnsilium Imperātōris adesse saepe iubeor. invītus pāreō;
quotiēns enim sententiam meam ā Domitiānō rogor, difficile est   *25*
mihi respondēre; turpe vidētur mentīrī, perīculōsum vēra loquī.
nam iussū istīus tyrannī multī bonī damnātī sunt.

    audīvistīne umquam poētam Valerium Mārtiālem
recitantem? ego quidem recitātiōnibus eius saepe adsum; tū sī
eum audīveris, certē dēlectāberis. versūs eius semper ēlegantēs,   *30*
nōnnumquam scurrīlēs sunt. eum tamen ideō reprehendō, quod
Imperātōrem nimium adulātur.

    quandō rūre discēdēs, mī Lupe? quandō iterum tē in urbe
vidēbimus? cum prīmum ad urbem redieris, mē vīsitā, quaesō;
sī tē mox vīderō, valdē dēlectābor. valē.   *35*

salūtem dīcit *sends good wishes*
quid agis? *how are you? how
   are you getting on?*
invideō: invidēre *envy*
ōtium *leisure*
officia: officium *duty*
prīvāta: prīvātus *private*
querēlārum: querēla
   complaint
triumphum … ēgit:
   triumphum agere *celebrate
   a triumph*
dē Germānīs *over the Germans*

patriae: patria *country,
   homeland*
litterae *letters, correspondence*
Calēdoniōs: Calēdoniī *Scots*
utrum … est … an? *is it … or?*
sēiūncta: sēiūnctus *separate*
cōnsilium *council*
turpe: turpis *shameful*
mentīrī *lie, tell a lie*
tyrannī: tyrannus *tyrant*
recitātiōnibus: recitātiō
   recital, public reading
nōnnumquam *sometimes*
ideō … quod *for the reason
   that, because*
reprehendō: reprehendere
   blame, criticise
adulātur: adulārī *flatter*
rūre: rūs *country, countryside*
cum prīmum *as soon as*
quaesō *I beg, i.e. please*

Questions

		Marks
1	Who is writing this letter? To whom is it written?	1
2	Where is Lupus?	1
3	**nam … quiēs** (lines 4–5). What is Glabrio complaining about here?	1
4	In lines 6–9 (**prīmā hōrā … pūblica agō**) Glabrio explains why he is so busy every day. Write down two of the reasons he gives.	2
5	**at tū … dēlectāris** (lines 9–11). How does Glabrio imagine that his friend is spending his time?	3
6	What public event has just taken place in Rome?	1
7	What two different reactions did it get from the people (lines 13–14)?	2
8	**'illī … haudquāquam Germānī sunt'** (lines 17–18). If they were not Germans, who did some people think they were?	2
9	What is going on in Britain (lines 20–1)?	1
10	What has Glabrio heard about the Scots?	1
11	What problem does Glabrio have about the geography of Scotland (line 23)?	2
12	What order does Glabrio often receive (line 24)?	1
13	Why does he find it difficult to give the Emperor his opinion (line 26)?	2
14	**versūs eius … adulātur** (lines 30–2). What is Glabrio's opinion of the work of the poet Martial?	3
15	What evidence is there in this letter to show that Glabrio and Lupus are close friends? Make two points.	2

TOTAL **25**

dum ego strepitū urbis vexor, tū carmine avium dēlectāris.

About the language 1: passive and deponent verbs

1   Study the following examples:

māne ā clientibus meīs **salūtor**.
*In the morning, **I am greeted** by my clients.*

Imperātōrem dērīsistī; sevērē nunc **pūnīris**.
*You mocked the Emperor; now **you are** severely **punished**.*

The words in **bold type** are passive forms of the 1st and 2nd persons singular.

2   Compare the active and passive forms of the 1st person singular in the following three tenses:

	active	*passive*
present	portō	portor
	I carry	*I am carried*
future	portābō	portābor
	I shall carry	*I shall be carried*
imperfect	portābam	portābar
	I was carrying	*I was being carried*

Further examples:

a   nunc ā cīvibus accūsor; crās laudābor.
b   ā medicō saepe vīsitābar, quod morbō gravī afflīgēbar.
c   doceor, invītābor, trahēbar, terrēbor, impediēbar, audior.

3   Compare the active and passive forms of the 2nd person singular:

	active	*passive*
present	portās	portāris
	you carry	*you are carried*
future	portābis	portāberis
	you will carry	*you will be carried*
imperfect	portābās	portābāris
	you were carrying	*you were being carried*

Further examples:

a   nōlī dēspērāre! mox līberāberis.
b   heri in carcere retinēbāris; hodiē ab Imperātōre honōrāris.
c   audīris, rogāberis, iubēbāris, monēris, trahēbāris, dēlectāberis.

4 Compare the 1st and 2nd person singular forms of **portō** with those of the deponent verb **cōnor**:

	active	*passive*	*deponent*
present	portō	portor	cōnor
	I carry	*I am carried*	*I try*
	portās	portāris	cōnāris
	you carry	*you are carried*	*you try*
future	portābō	portābor	cōnābor
	I shall carry	*I shall be carried*	*I shall try*
	portābis	portāberis	cōnāberis
	you will carry	*you will be carried*	*you will try*
imperfect	portābam	portābar	cōnābar
	I was carrying	*I was being carried*	*I was trying*
	portābās	portābāris	cōnābāris
	you were carrying	*you were being carried*	*you were trying*

Further examples of 1st and 2nd person singular forms of deponent verbs:

a crās deam precābor.
b cūr domum meam ingrediēbāris?
c hortor, hortāris, suspicābor, suspicāberis, sequēbar, sequēbāris.

One of the most enjoyable times in the rural year – gathering the grapes for wine-making and treading them to press out the juice (right).

vīta rūstica

C. Helvidius Lupus salūtem dīcit Acīliō Glabriōnī amīcō.
cum epistulam tuam legerem, mī Glabriō, gaudium et dolōrem
simul sēnsī. gaudiō enim afficiēbar, quod tam diū epistulam ā tē
exspectābam; dolēbam autem, quod tū tot labōribus
opprimēbāris.   5

    in epistulā tuā dīcis tē valdē occupātum esse. ego quoque,
cum Rōmae essem, saepe negōtiīs vexābar; nunc tamen vītā
rūsticā dēlector. aliquandō per agrōs meōs equitō; aliquandō
fundum īnspiciō. crās in silvīs proximīs vēnābor; vīcīnī enim
crēdunt aprum ingentem ibi latēre. nōn tamen omnīnō ōtiōsus   10
sum; nam sīcut tū ā clientibus tuīs salūtāris atque vexāris, ita ego
ā colōnīs meīs assiduē vexor.

    rēctē dīcis Calēdoniōs omnium Britannōrum ferōcissimōs
esse. amīcus meus Sīlānus, quī cum Agricolā in Britanniā nūper
mīlitābat, dīcit Calēdoniōs in ultimīs partibus Britanniae   15
habitāre, inter saxa et undās. quamquam Calēdoniī ferōcissimē
pugnāre solent, Sīlānus affirmat exercitum nostrum eōs vincere
posse. crēdit enim Rōmānōs nōn modo multō fortiōrēs esse
quam Calēdoniōs, sed etiam ducem meliōrem habēre.

    dē poētā Mārtiāle tēcum cōnsentiō: inest in eō multum   20
ingenium, multa ars. ego vērō ōlim versibus Ovidiī poētae
maximē dēlectābar; nunc tamen mihi epigrammata Mārtiālis
magis placent.

    in epistulā tuā Helvidium, fīlium meum, commemorās. quem
tamen rārissimē videō! nam in hāc vīllā trēs diēs mēcum   25
morātus, ad urbem rediit; suspicor eum puellam aliquam in

dolēbam: dolēre *grieve, be sad*

vēnābor: vēnārī *hunt*
vīcīnī: vīcīnus *neighbour*
sīcut … ita *just as … so*
colōnīs: colōnus *tenant-farmer*
rēctē *rightly*

affirmat: affirmāre *declare*

vērō *indeed*
epigrammata: epigramma
   epigram

aliquam: aliquī *some*

sīcut tū ā clientibus tuīs
salūtāris atque vexāris, ita ego
ā colōnīs meīs assiduē vexor.

urbe vīsitāre. quīndecim iam annōs nātus est; nihil cūrat nisi puellās et quadrīgās. difficile autem est mihi eum culpāre; nam ego quoque, cum iuvenis essem – sed satis nūgārum!

nunc tū mihi graviter admonendus es, mī Glabriō. in epistulā 30 tuā dē quōdam virō potentī male scrībis, quem nōmināre nōlō. tibi cavendum est, mī amīce! perīculōsum est dē potentibus male scrībere. virī potentēs celeriter īrāscuntur, lentē molliuntur. nisi cāveris, mī Glabriō, damnāberis atque occīdēris. sollicitus haec scrībō; salūs enim tua mihi magnae cūrae est. valē. 35

quadrīgās: quadrīga *chariot*
nūgārum: nūgae *nonsense, foolish talk*
admonendus es: admonēre *warn, advise*
male *badly, unfavourably*
nōmināre *name, mention by name*
īrāscuntur: īrāscī *become angry*

A country farm

This small farm (**vīlla rūstica**) at Boscoreale, near Pompeii, was buried by Vesuvius in AD 79. It was possible for the archaeologists to trace the holes where the vines were planted and vines have now been planted there again. The wine was fermented in buried jars (below), which were then covered with lids to store it.

Farmers were recommended to have enough jars to store their wine for up to five years, so as to sell at the time when prices were highest.

The owner of this sort of farm would probably have let it out to a tenant (**colōnus**) to run.

About the language 2: indirect statement

1   In Book I, you met sentences like these:

> 'mercātor multam pecūniam habet.'   'servī cibum parant.'
> *The merchant has a lot of money.'*   *'The slaves are preparing the food.'*

In each example, a statement is being *made*. These examples are known as direct statements. Notice the nouns **mercātor** and **servī** and the verbs **habet** and **parant**.

2   In Stage 35, you have met sentences like these:

> scīmus **mercātōrem** multam pecūniam **habēre**.
> *We know the merchant to have a lot of money.*
> Or, in more natural English:
> *We know that the merchant has a lot of money.*

> crēdō **servōs** cibum **parāre**.
> *I believe the slaves to be preparing the food.*
> Or, in more natural English:
> *I believe that the slaves are preparing the food.*

In each of these examples, the statement is not being made, but is being *reported* or *mentioned*. These examples are known as indirect statements. Notice that the nouns **mercātōrem** and **servōs** are now in the *accusative* case, and the verbs **habēre** and **parāre** are now in the *infinitive* form.

3   Compare the following examples:

direct statements	*indirect statements*
'captīvī dormiunt.'	centuriō dīcit **captīvōs dormīre**.
'The prisoners are asleep.'	*The centurion says that the prisoners are asleep.*
'Lupus in vīllā rūsticā habitat.'	audiō **Lupum** in vīllā rūsticā **habitāre**.
'Lupus is living in his country villa.'	*I hear that Lupus is living in his country villa.*

4   Further examples of direct and indirect statements:

    a 'hostēs appropinquant.'
    b nūntius dīcit hostēs appropinquāre.
    c 'Agricola bellum in Calēdoniā gerit.'
    d audiō Agricolam bellum in Calēdoniā gerere.
    e rhētor affirmat fīlium meum dīligenter labōrāre.
    f dominus crēdit fugitīvōs in silvā latēre.
    g scīmus mīlitēs nostrōs semper fortiter pugnāre.
    h dīcisne patrōnum tuum esse virum līberālem?

Word patterns: compounds of faciō, capiō and iaciō

1 Study the following pairs of verbs and note how **faciō**, **capiō** and **iaciō** change when a preposition or prefix such as **per** or **re-** is put in front of them.

faciō	facere	fēcī	factus	*make, do*
perficiō	perficere	perfēcī	perfectus	*finish*
capiō	capere	cēpī	captus	*take*
recipiō	recipere	recēpī	receptus	*take back, recover*
iaciō	iacere	iēcī	iactus	*throw*
ēicio	ēicere	ēiēcī	ēiectus	*throw out*

2 Using paragraph 1 as a guide, complete the table below.

dēiciō	. . . .	dēiēcī	. . . .	*throw down*
. . . .	afficere	affēcī	. . . .	*affect*
suscipiō	. . . .	. . . .	susceptus	*undertake*
iniciō	. . . .	. . . .	. . . .	. . . .

3 Using the paragraphs above, find the Latin for:

to recover; I am undertaking; I have finished; having been thrown down.

4 The following verbs have occurred in checklists:

efficiō, incipiō, coniciō.

Using the table in paragraph 1, can you write out their four parts and give their meanings?

Tenants bringing gifts to the villa owner.

Practising the language

1 Complete each sentence with the most suitable verb from the box below, using the correct form of the future tense. Then translate the sentence. Do not use any verb more than once.

| terrēbit | reficiet | dabit | pugnābit | dūcet |
| terrēbunt | reficient | dabunt | pugnābunt | dūcent |

   a hī fabrī sunt perītissimī; nāvem tuam celeriter . . . .
   b crās dominus lībertātem duōbus servīs . . . .
   c leōnēs, quī ferōciōrēs sunt quam cēterae bēstiae, spectātōrēs fortasse . . . .
   d sī templum vīsitāre vīs, hic servus tē illūc . . . .
   e frāter meus, gladiātor nōtissimus, crās in amphitheātrō . . . .

2 Turn each of the following pairs into one sentence by replacing the word in **bold type** with the correct form of the relative pronoun **quī**, **quae**, **quod**. Use paragraph 1 on p. 113 to help you. Then translate the sentence.

   For example: prō templō erant duo virī. **virōs** statim agnōvī.
   This becomes: prō templō erant duo virī, **quōs** statim agnōvī.
                  *In front of the temple were two men, **whom** I recognised at once.*

   a in fundō nostrō sunt vīgintī servī. **servī** in agrīs cotīdiē labōrant.
   b in hāc vīllā habitat lībertus. **lībertum** vīsitāre volō.
   c prope iānuam stābat fēmina. **fēminae** epistulam trādidī.
   d audī illam puellam! **puella** suāviter cantat.
   e in viā erant multī puerī. **puerōrum** clāmōrēs senem vexābant.
   f vīdistīne templum? **templum** nūper aedificātum est.

3 Select the participle which agrees with the noun in **bold type**. Then translate the sentence.

   a **hospitēs**, dōna pretiōsissima . . . ., ad vīllam prīncipis contendēbant. (ferentēs, ferentia)
   b versūs **poētae**, in forō . . . ., ab omnibus audītī erant. (recitantis, recitantium)
   c **pecūniā** . . . ., fūr in silvam cucurrit. (raptā, raptō, raptīs)
   d **sacerdōtibus**, ē templō . . . ., victimās ostendimus. (ēgressōs, ēgressīs)
   e **nāvēs**, in lītore . . . ., īnspicere volēbam. (īnstrūcta, īnstrūctae, īnstrūctās)
   f **puer**, canem . . . ., arborem quam celerrimē cōnscendit. (cōnspicātus, cōnspicāta, cōnspicātum)
   g fēminae **mīlitēs** vīdērunt captīvum . . . . (pulsantem, pulsātōs, pulsātūrōs)
   h puella nesciēbat cūr **pater** ancillam . . . . esset. (pūnītūrus, pūnītūra, pūnītūram)

Country villas

Many wealthy Romans, like Lupus on pp. 2–7, owned both a town house in Rome and at least one villa in the country. There they could escape from the noise and heat of the city, especially during the unhealthy months of late summer, and relax from the pressures of private business and public duties.

Some of these country houses were fairly close to Rome; their owners could get a day's work done in the city and then travel out to their villa before nightfall. The villas were generally either on the coast, like Pliny's villa at Laurentum, or on the hills around Rome, for example at Tibur, where the Emperor Hadrian owned the most spectacular mansion of all, surrounded by specially constructed imitations of buildings that had impressed him on his travels.

An emperor's villa

Hadrian's villa near Tibur, 19 miles from Rome: a vast, sprawling complex covering 300 acres (120 hectares). The photograph of the model shows only part of it.

There were two theatres and three bath buildings; huge state rooms contrasted with more homely quarters for the emperor's private use. He loved to enjoy the landscape. A terrace (top, foreground) has views over a valley he called the Vale of Tempe after a famous Greek beauty spot. An outdoor dining-room (below) looks over a canal which may have recalled the Canopus at Alexandria.

Other country villas were further afield. A popular area was Campania; the coastline of the bay of Naples was dotted with the villas of wealthy men, while holiday resorts such as Baiae had a reputation for fast living and immorality.

Country villas naturally varied in design, but they usually contained some or all of the following features: a series of dining and reception rooms for entertaining guests, often with extensive views of the surrounding countryside; a set of baths, heated by hypocausts, containing the full range of apodyterium, tepidarium, caldarium and frigidarium; long colonnades where the owner and his friends might walk, or even ride, sheltered from the rain or from the direct heat of the sun; and extensive parkland, farmland or gardens, preferably with plenty of shade and running water. In a corner of the estate there might be a small shrine, dedicated to the protecting gods.

Pliny's letters include descriptions of two of his villas. Although detailed, the descriptions are not always clear, and many scholars have tried to reconstruct the plans of the villas, without reaching agreement. An attempt at the plan of Pliny's Laurentine villa is shown below, together with a model based on the plan. Among the villa's special features were the heated swimming-pool (10), the big semi-circular recess at the end of the chief dining-room (4), designed to provide the dinner guests with an impressive panorama of the sea, and the covered colonnade (12) leading to Pliny's private suite (14). This suite

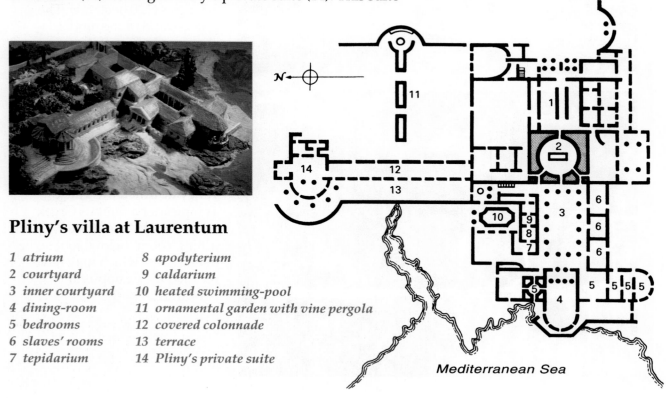

Pliny's villa at Laurentum

1 atrium
2 courtyard
3 inner courtyard
4 dining-room
5 bedrooms
6 slaves' rooms
7 tepidarium
8 apodyterium
9 caldarium
10 heated swimming-pool
11 ornamental garden with vine pergola
12 covered colonnade
13 terrace
14 Pliny's private suite

Mediterranean Sea

was Pliny's own addition to the building, and it provided him with quiet and privacy; at the noisy mid-winter festival of the Saturnalia, for example, Pliny could retire to his suite while his slaves enjoyed themselves in the main villa, so that he did not get in the way of their celebrations and they did not disturb his peace.

Country pursuits

One of the most popular recreations for a wealthy Roman on his country estate was hunting. Hares, deer or wild boar were tracked down and chased into nets where they could be speared to death. Long ropes, to which brightly coloured feathers were attached, were slung from trees to cut off the animal's retreat and frighten it back towards the nets. The actual chasing was often left to slaves and dogs, while the hunter contented himself with waiting at the nets and spearing the boar or deer when it had become thoroughly entangled. Pliny, for example, in reporting a successful expedition on which he caught three boars, says that he took his stilus and writing-tablets with him to the hunt and jotted down ideas under the inspiration of the woodland scene while he waited for the boars to appear. But although Pliny's description of hunting is a very peaceful one, the sport still had its dangers: a cornered boar might turn on its pursuers, and a hunter who was slow with his spear might be gashed severely, even fatally.

The hunter (bottom left) has been gored by the cornered boar.

Fishing also seems to have been popular, and could easily be combined with rowing or sailing, either on the sea (in the bay of Naples, for example) or on such lakes as the Lucrine lake, famous for its fish and its oysters. A lazier method of fishing is described by Martial, who refers to a villa with a bedroom directly overlooking the sea, so that the occupant could drop a fishing-line from the window and catch a fish without even getting out of bed.

Some of Pliny's letters describe his daily routine at his country villas. He spent most of his time in gentle exercise (walking, riding or occasionally hunting), working on a speech or other piece of writing, dealing with his tenant-farmers (**colōnī**), entertaining friends, dining, or listening to a reading or to music. He often spent part of the afternoon reading a Greek or Latin speech aloud 'for the sake of both voice and digestion'. (Pliny often spoke in the law courts and the senate, and he was naturally anxious to keep his voice in good trim.)

The economy of the villa

A country villa of this kind, however, was not just for holiday relaxation: it was an important investment. Often there was a farm attached to the house, and the property would usually include an extensive area of land which the owner might farm himself or lease to tenant-farmers. In the ancient world, by far the commonest way of investing money was to buy land. It is not surprising that many of Pliny's letters deal with the day-to-day problems of land management. He agonises over whether to buy a neighbouring piece of land, fertile and conveniently situated but long neglected; he asks the emperor to excuse him from Rome so that he can be on one of his estates at a time when the tenancy is changing hands; and when his tenants get into difficulties and are heavily in debt, he arranges for them to pay their rent with part of their crops rather than in cash. He likes to present himself as an ignorant amateur with no interest in the running of his villas, but some of his comments give the impression that he was in fact enthusiastic, practical and shrewd. One of his villas brought him an income of 400,000 sesterces a year. If you compare this with the annual pay of a centurion – about 6,000 sesterces a year – and remember that Pliny owned other villas and property, you can see that he was a very successful landowner.

Tenants paying their rent.

What country activities can you find in this picture?

Vocabulary checklist 35

ager, agrī	field
an	or
utrum … an	whether … or
carmen, carminis	song
caveō, cavēre, cāvī	beware
culpō, culpāre, culpāvī	blame
inde	then
magis	more
male	badly, unfavourably
moror, morārī, morātus sum	delay
multō	much
nusquam	nowhere
quandō?	when?
quidem	indeed
quotiēns	whenever
rūs, rūris	country, countryside
simul	at the same time

A grand country villa, with symmetrical wings and a formal garden in front. A painting in Pompeii.

RECITATIO

STAGE 36

Marcus Valerius Mārtiālis

I

in audītōriō exspectant multī cīvēs. adsunt ut Valerium Mārtiālem,
poētam nōtissimum, recitantem audiant. omnēs inter sē colloquuntur.
subitō signum datur ut taceant; audītōrium intrat poēta ipse.
audītōribus plaudentibus, Mārtiālis scaenam ascendit ut versūs suōs
recitet.   5

Mārtiālis: salvēte, amīcī. (*librum ēvolvit.*) prīmum
                    recitāre volō versūs quōsdam nūper dē
                    Sabidiō compositōs.

complūrēs audītōrēs sē convertunt ut Sabidium, quī in ultimō sellārum
ōrdine sedet, spectent.   10

Mārtiālis: nōn amo tē, Sabidī, nec possum dīcere quārē.
                     hoc tantum possum dīcere – nōn amo tē.

audītor: (*cum amīcīs susurrāns*) illōs versūs nōn
                    intellegō. cūr poēta dīcere nōn potest quārē
                    Sabidium nōn amet?   15
prīmus amīcus: (*susurrāns*) scīlicet poēta ipse causam nescit.
secundus amīcus: (*susurrāns*) minimē, poēta optimē scit quārē
                    Sabidium nōn amet: sed tam foeda est causa
                    ut poēta eam patefacere nōlit.
aliī audītōrēs: st! st!   20

audītōriō: audītōrium
   auditorium, hall (used for
   public readings)
colloquuntur: colloquī *talk,*
   chat
audītōribus: audītor *listener,*
   (pl.) audience
ēvolvit: ēvolvere *unroll, open*
compositōs: compōnere
   compose, make up
complūrēs *several*

st! *hush!*

prīmus amīcus:	hem! audītōrēs nōbīs imperant ut taceāmus.
Mārtiālis:	nunc dē Laecāniā et Thāide, fēminīs
	'nōtissimīs': (audītōrēs sibi rīdent.)

Thāide *ablative of* Thāis

	Thāis habet **nigrōs**, niveōs Laecānia **dentēs**.*	
	quae ratiō est? . . .	25
audītor:	(*interpellāns*) . . . ēmptōs haec habet, illa suōs!	

quae?: quī? *what?*
ratiō *reason*
haec ... illa *this one (Laecania)*
  ... *that one (Thais)*

Mārtiālis, valdē īrātus, dē scaenā dēscendit ut audītōrem vituperet.

Mārtiālis:	ego poēta sum, tū tantum audītor. ego hūc	
	invītātus sum ut recitem, tū ut audiās.	
	(*subitō audītōrem agnōscit.*) hem! sciō quis sīs.	30
	tū Pontiliānus es, quī semper mē rogās ut	
	libellōs meōs tibi mittam. at nunc, mī	
	Pontiliāne, tibi dīcere possum quārē semper	
	mittere recūsem. (*ad scaenam reversus,*	
	recitātiōnem renovat.)	35

renovat: renovāre *continue,*
  resume

	cūr nōn mittō **meōs** tibi, Pontiliāne, **libellōs**?
	nē mihi tū mittās, Pontiliāne, tuōs!

omnēs praeter Pontiliānum rīdent. Pontiliānus autem tam īrātus est ut
ē sellā surgat. ad scaenam sē praecipitāre cōnātur ut Mārtiālem pulset,
sed amīcī eum retinent.   40

*Some noun-and-adjective phrases, in which an adjective is separated by one
word or more from the noun which it describes, are shown in **bold type**.

II

Mārtiālis, quī iam ūnam hōram recitat, ad fīnem librī appropinquat.

Mārtiālis:	postrēmō pauca dē prīncipe nostrō, Domitiānō Augustō, dīcere velim. aliquōs versūs nūper dē illā aulā ingentī composuī quae in monte Palātīnō stat:

> aethera contingit **nova** nostrī prīncipis **aula**;
> clārius in **tōtō** sōl videt **orbe** nihil.
> **haec**, Auguste, tamen, quae vertice sīdera pulsat,
> pār **domus** est caelō sed minor est dominō.

plūrimī audītōrēs vehementissimē plaudunt; animadvertunt enim Epaphrodītum, Domitiānī lībertum, in audītōriō adesse. ūnus audītor tamen, M'. Acīlius Glabriō, tālī adulātiōne offēnsus, nōn modo plausū abstinet sed ē sellā surgit et ex audītōriō exit. quā audāciā attonitus, Mārtiālis paulīsper immōtus stat; deinde ad extrēmam scaenam prōcēdit ut plausum excipiat. ūnus tamen audītor exclāmat:

audītor:	sed quid dē mē, Mārtiālis? epigramma dē mē compōnere nunc potes?
Mārtiālis:	dē tē, homuncule? quis es et quālis?
audītor:	nōmine Diaulus sum. artem medicīnae nūper exercēbam …
alius audītor:	… at nunc vespillō es!

omnēs rīdent; rīdet praesertim Mārtiālis.

Mārtiālis:	bene! nunc epigramma accipe, mī Diaule:

> nūper erat medicus, nunc est vespillo Diaulus.
> quod vespillo facit, fēcerat et medicus.

cachinnant multī; ērubēscit Diaulus. Mārtiālis, recitātiōne ita perfectā, ex audītōriō ēgreditur, omnibus praeter Diaulum plaudentibus. servī ingressī audītōribus vīnum cibumque offerunt.

prīncipe: prīnceps *emperor*

monte Palātīnō: mōns Palātīnus *the Palatine hill*

aethera *accusative of* **aethēr** *sky, heaven*

contingit: contingere *touch*

clārius … nihil *nothing more splendid*

orbe: orbis *globe, world*

vertice: vertex *top, peak*

sīdera: sīdus *star*

pār *equal*

minor … dominō *smaller than its master*

M'. = Mānius

adulātiōne: adulātiō *flattery*

abstinet: abstinēre *abstain*

ad extrēmam scaenam *to the edge of the stage*

vespillō *undertaker*

quod = id quod *what*
et = etiam *also*

The Emperor Domitian's palace overlooking the Circus Maximus.

About the language 1: present subjunctive

1   In Book III, you met the imperfect and pluperfect tenses of the subjunctive:

> *imperfect*
> haruspex aderat ut victimam **īnspiceret**.
> *The soothsayer was there in order that he might examine the victim.*
>   Or, in more natural English:
>   *The soothsayer was there to examine the victim.*
>
> *pluperfect*
> rēx prīncipēs rogāvit num hostēs **vīdissent**.
> *The king asked the chieftains whether they had seen the enemy.*

2   In Stage 36, you have met sentences like these:

> cīvēs conveniunt ut poētam **audiant**.
> *The citizens are gathering in order that they may hear the poet.*
>   Or, in more natural English:
>   *The citizens are gathering to hear the poet.*
>
> Mārtiālis dīcere nōn potest quārē Sabidium nōn **amet**.
> *Martial is unable to say why he does not like Sabidius.*

The form of the verb in **bold type** is the present subjunctive.

3   Further examples:

  a   cognōscere volō quid illī fabrī aedificent.
  b   tam saevus est dominus noster ut servōs semper pūniat.
  c   in agrīs cotīdiē labōrō ut cibum līberīs meīs praebeam.
  d   nōn intellegimus quārē tālī hominī crēdās.

4   Compare the present subjunctive with the present indicative:

	present indicative *(3rd person singular and plural)*		*present subjunctive* *(3rd person singular and plural)*	
first conjugation	portat	portant	portet	portent
second conjugation	docet	docent	doceat	doceant
third conjugation	trahit	trahunt	trahat	trahant
fourth conjugation	audit	audiunt	audiat	audiant

The present subjunctive of all four conjugations is set out in full on p. 118 of the Language Information section.

5   For the present subjunctive of irregular verbs, see p. 123.

epigrammata Mārtiālia

The following epigrams, and also the ones which appeared on
pp. 18–20, were written by Marcus Valerius Martialis (Martial)
and published between AD 86 and 101.

I *dē Tuccā, quī saepe postulat ut Mārtiālis libellōs sibi dōnet*
        exigis ut **nostrōs** dōnem tibi, Tucca, **libellōs**.
           nōn faciam: nam vīs vēndere, nōn legere.

> **dōnet: dōnāre** *give*
> **exigis: exigere** *demand*
> **nostrōs: noster = meus** *my*

Why does Martial refuse Tucca's demand?

II *dē Sextō, iuvene glōriōsō*
        dīcis amōre tuī **bellās** ardēre **puellās**,
           quī faciem sub aquā, Sexte, natantis habēs.

> **glōriōsō: glōriōsus** *boastful*
> **bellās: bellus** *pretty*
> **faciem: faciēs** *face*

Judging from Martial's description, what impression do you
have of Sextus' appearance?

III *dē Symmachō medicō discipulīsque eius centum*
        languēbam: sed tū comitātus prōtinus ad mē
           vēnistī **centum**, Symmache, **discipulīs**.
        centum mē tetigēre **manūs** Aquilōne **gelātae**;
           nōn habuī febrem, Symmache: nunc habeō.

> **discipulīs: discipulus** *pupil,*
>   *student*
> **languēbam: languēre** *feel*
>   *weak, feel ill*
> **prōtinus** *immediately*
> **tetigēre = tetigērunt: tangere**
>   *touch*
> **Aquilōne: Aquilō** *North wind*
> **gelātae: gelāre** *freeze*
> **febrem: febris** *fever*

Why do you think Martial repeats the word **centum** (lines
2–3) and uses the phrase **Aquilōne gelātae** (line 3)?

*centum mē tetigēre manūs
Aquilōne gelātae.*

IV *dē Catullō, quī saepe dīcit Mārtiālem hērēdem sibi esse*

> hērēdem tibi mē, Catulle, dīcis.
> non crēdam nisi lēgerō, Catulle.

When will Martial believe Catullus' promise? Why do you
think he will believe it then, but not believe it earlier?

V *dē Quīntō, quī Thāida lūscam amat*

> 'Thāida Quīntus amat.' 'quam Thāida?' 'Thāida lūscam.'
> ūnum oculum Thāis nōn habet, ille duōs.

Thāida *accusative of* **Thāis**
lūscam: lūscus *one-eyed*
quam?: quī? *which?*

What do the last two words suggest about
a Quintus **b** Thais?

VI *dē Vacerrā, quī veterēs poētās sōlōs mīrātur*

> mīrāris **veterēs**, Vacerra, sōlōs
> nec laudās nisi mortuōs **poētās**.
> ignōscās petimus, Vacerra: tantī
> nōn est, ut placeam tibī, perīre.

mīrātur: mīrārī *admire*
**ignōscās petimus = petimus
ut nōbīs ignōscās**
tantī nōn est … perīre *it is not
worth dying*

Do people like Vacerra still exist nowadays?

*Christ shown as a Roman reading
from a book.*

About the language 2: word order

1   From Stage 3 onwards, you have met phrases in which an adjective is placed next to the noun it describes:

ad **silvam obscūram**   *to the dark wood*
contrā **multōs barbarōs**   *against many barbarians*
in **flūmine altō**   *in the deep river*

2   In Book III, you met phrases in which an adjective is separated by a preposition from the noun which it describes:

tōtam per **urbem**   *through the whole city*
omnibus cum **mīlitibus**   *with all the soldiers*
hōc ex **oppidō**   *from this town*

3   In Stage 36, you have met sentences like these:

cūr nōn mitto **meōs** tibi, Pontiliāne, **libellōs**?
Why do I not send you my writings, Pontilianus?

aethera contingit **nova** nostrī prīncipis **aula**.
The new palace of our emperor touches the sky.

This kind of word order, in which an adjective is separated by one or more words from the noun which it describes, is particularly common in verse.

Further examples:

a   dēnique centuriō **magnam** pervēnit ad **urbem**.
b   nox erat, et **caelō** fulgēbat lūna **serēnō**. (*From a poem by Horace*)
c   flūminis in rīpā nunc **noster** dormit **amīcus**.

4   In each of the following examples, pick out the Latin adjective and say which noun it is describing:

a   atque iterum ad Trōiam magnus mittētur Achillēs. (*Virgil*)
And great Achilles will be sent again to Troy.
b   ergō sollicitae tū causa, pecūnia, vītae! (*Propertius*)
Therefore you, money, are the cause of an anxious life!
c   rōbustus quoque iam taurīs iuga solvet arātor. (*Virgil*)
Now, too, the strong ploughman will unfasten the yoke from the bulls.

5 Translate the following examples:

a *On a journey*
cōnspicimus montēs atque altae moenia Rōmae.
b *Cries of pain*
clāmōrēs simul horrendōs ad sīdera tollit. (*Virgil*)
c *A foreigner*
hic posuit nostrā nūper in urbe pedem. (*Propertius*)
d *Preparations for battle*
tum iuvenis validā sustulit arma manū.
e *The foolishness of sea travel*
cūr cupiunt nautae saevās properāre per undās?

moenia *city walls*
horrendōs: horrendus *horrifying*
properāre *hurry*

Pick out the adjective in each example and say which noun it is describing.

Word patterns: adjectives ending in -ōsus

1 Study the following nouns and adjectives:

perīculum	*danger*	perīculōsus	*dangerous*
pretium	*price, value*	pretiōsus	*valuable*
fōrma	*beauty*	fōrmōsus	*beautiful*

2 Now complete the table below:

ōtium	*leisure*	....	*idle, at leisure*
spatium	*space*	spatiōsus	....
herba	....	herbōsus	*grassy*
glōria	*glory, pride*	....	*glorious, boasting*
odium	....	....	*hateful*

3 Match the adjectives in the box with the meanings below:

perfidiōsus	furiōsus	ventōsus
fūmōsus	iocōsus	annōsus

windy	....	treacherous	....
raging, mad	....	old	....
smoky	....	fond of jokes	....

Practising the language

1 Complete each sentence with the correct verb. Then translate the sentence.

    a Mārtiālis versum dē Imperātōre compōnere . . . . (cōnābātur, ēgrediēbātur)

    b mīlitēs ducem ad ultimās regiōnēs Britanniae . . . . (sequēbantur, suspicābantur)

    c omnēs senātōrēs dē victōriā Agricolae . . . . (adipīscēbantur, loquēbantur)

    d cūr amīcum . . . . ut ad urbem revenīret? (cōnspicābāris, hortābāris)

    e clientēs, quī patrōnum ad forum . . . ., viam complēbant. (comitābantur, proficīscēbantur)

    f nēmō mē, quī multōs cāsūs . . . ., adiuvāre volēbat. (patiēbar, precābar)

2 Translate each sentence. Then change the words in **bold type** from singular to plural. Use the tables on pp. 104–13 and 122 to help you.

    a tribūnus **centuriōnem callidum** laudāvit.

    b frāter meus, postquam **hoc templum** vīdit, admīrātiōne affectus est.

    c senex **amīcō dēspērantī** auxilium tulit.

    d ubi **est puella**? **eam** salūtāre volō.

    e iuvenis, **hastā ingentī** armātus, aprum saevum petīvit.

    f **puer, quem** heri pūnīvī, hodiē labōrāre nōn **potest**.

    g mē iubēs **rem difficilem** facere.

    h mīlitēs **flūmen altum** trānsiērunt.

3 Complete each sentence with the most suitable verb from the box below, using the correct form. Then translate the sentence. Do not use any verb more than once.

occīdit	accēpit	iussit	recitāvit	dūxit
occīdērunt	accēpērunt	iussērunt	recitāvērunt	dūxērunt
occīsus est	acceptus est	iussus est	recitātus est	ductus est
occīsī sunt	acceptī sunt	iussī sunt	recitātī sunt	ductī sunt

    a senātor ā servō . . . .

    b poēta multōs versūs dē Imperātōre . . . .

    c captīvī per viās urbis in triumphō . . . .

    d clientēs pecūniam laetissimē . . . .

    e lībertus ad aulam contendere . . . .

Recitātiōnēs

The easiest and commonest way for a Roman author to bring his work to the notice of the public was to read it aloud to them. For example, a poet might choose a convenient spot, such as a street corner, a barber's shop, or a colonnade in the forum, and recite his poems to anyone who cared to stop and listen. Like any kind of street performance or sales talk, this could be very entertaining or very annoying for the passers-by. In an exaggerated but colourful complaint, Martial claims that a poet called Ligurinus used to recite continually at him, whether he was eating dinner, hurrying along the street, swimming in the baths, or using the public lavatories, and that even when he went to sleep, Ligurinus woke him up and began reciting again.

An author reading from a scroll.

Often, however, a writer's work received its first reading in a more comfortable place than the street corner, with a carefully chosen group of listeners rather than a casual collection of passers-by. A natural audience for a writer was his patron, if he had one, and his patron's family and friends. For example, Virgil read sections of his poem the *Aeneid* to the Emperor Augustus and to Augustus' sister Octavia, who is said to have fainted when Virgil reached a part of the poem which referred to her dead son Marcellus. A writer might also invite friends to his house and read his work to them there, perhaps inviting them to make comments or criticisms before he composed a final version of the work. This kind of reading sometimes took place at a dinner party. If the host was an accomplished and entertaining writer, this would add to the guests' enjoyment of the meal; but some hosts made great nuisances of themselves by reading boring or poor-quality work.

Mosaic showing the poet Virgil, with the Aeneid *on his lap. The two female figures are goddesses, the Muses of epic poetry and tragedy.*

The public reading of a writer's work often took place at a special occasion known as a **recitātiō**, like the one on pp. 18–20, in which an invited audience had a chance to hear the author's work and could decide whether or not to buy a copy or have a copy made. The recitatio might be given at the writer's house, or more often the house of his patron; or a hall (**audītōrium**) might be specially hired for the purpose. Invitations were sent out. Cushioned chairs were set out at the front for the more distinguished guests; benches were placed behind them, and, if the recitatio was a very grand occasion, tiered seats on temporary scaffolding. Slaves gave out programmes to the audience as they arrived, and if the writer was unscrupulous or over-anxious, one or two friends might be stationed at particular points in the audience with instructions to applaud at the right moments.

When all was ready, the reading started. Generally the author himself read his work, though there were exceptions. (Pliny, for example, knew that he was bad at reading poetry; so although he read his speeches himself, he had his poems read by a freedman.) The writer, specially dressed for the occasion in a freshly laundered toga, stepped forward and delivered a short introduction (**praefātiō**) to his work, then sat to read the work itself. The recital might be continued on a second and third day, sometimes at the request of the audience.

Things did not always go smoothly at recitationes. The Emperor Claudius, when young, embarked on a series of readings from his own historical work, but disaster struck when an enormously fat man joined the audience and sat down on a flimsy bench, which collapsed beneath him; in the general laughter it became impossible for the reading to continue. Pliny records a more serious incident during the reign of Trajan. A historian, who had announced that he would continue his reading in a few days' time, was approached by a group of people who begged him not to read the next instalment because they knew it would be dealing with some fairly recent events in which they had been concerned, and which they did not want read out in public. It is possible that the author concerned was the historian Tacitus, describing the misdeeds of the Emperor Domitian and his associates. The historian granted the request and cancelled the next instalment of the reading. However, as Pliny pointed out, cancelling the recitatio did not mean that the men's misdeeds would stay unknown: people would be all the more curious to read the history, in order to find out why the recitatio had been cancelled.

Pliny, who gave recitationes of his own work and also regularly attended those of other people, was very shocked at the frivolous way in which some members of the audience behaved: 'Some of them loiter and linger outside the hall, and send their slaves in to find out how far the recitatio has got; then, when the slaves report that the author has nearly finished his reading, they come in at last – and even then they don't always stay, but slip out before the end, some of them sheepishly and furtively, others boldly and brazenly.'

Some Roman writers are very critical of recitationes. Seneca, for example, says that when the author says to the audience 'Shall I read some more?' they usually reply 'Yes, please do', but privately they are praying for the man to be struck dumb. Juvenal sarcastically includes recitationes among the dangers and disadvantages of life in Rome, together with fires and falling buildings. In fact, the work read out must have varied enormously in quality: occasional masterpieces, a sprinkling of competent work and plenty of rubbish. A more serious criticism of recitationes is that they encouraged writers to think too much about impressing their audience. One author admitted: 'Much of

Statuette of a man reading from a scroll. With his prominent ears, he could have been intended as a caricature of Claudius.

what I say is said not because it pleases me but because it will please my hearers.'

However, in first-century Rome, when every copy of a book had to be produced individually by hand, recitationes filled a real need. They enabled the author to bring his work to the notice of many people without the expense and labour of creating large numbers of copies. Recitationes were also useful from the audience's point of view. It was far harder in Roman than in modern times to go into a bookshop, run one's eye over the titles and covers, sample the contents of a few likely-looking books, and make one's choice. The physical nature of a Roman book (see illustrations on pp. 23, 28 and overleaf) meant that there was no such thing as a cover; the title was printed not on a convenient part of the book but on a label attached to it, which was often lost; and the act of unrolling and reading a book, then re-rolling it ready for the next reader, was so laborious that sampling and browsing were virtually impossible. The recitatio allowed the author to present his work to an audience conveniently, economically and (if he was a good reader) interestingly.

A reconstruction of a Roman gentleman's library, with cupboards for the scrolls and a statue of Minerva, goddess of wisdom.

Vocabulary checklist 36

animadvertō, animadvertere, animadvertī, animadversus	*notice, take notice of*
arma, armōrum	*arms, weapons*
causa, causae	*reason, cause*
discipulus, discipulī	*pupil, student*
dōnō, dōnāre, dōnāvī, dōnātus	*give*
extrēmus, extrēma, extrēmum	*furthest*
fīnis, fīnis	*end*
ignis, ignis	*fire*
mīror, mīrārī, mīrātus sum	*admire, wonder at*
nē	*that … not, in order that … not*
niger, nigra, nigrum	*black*
praesertim	*especially*
praeter	*except*
recitō, recitāre, recitāvī, recitātus	*recite, read out*
tangō, tangere, tetigī, tāctus	*touch*
vetus, *gen.* veteris	*old*

Inkwell, pen and scroll, showing its label.

CONSILIUM

STAGE 37

Agricola, Calēdoniīs victīs, epistulam nūntiō dictat. in hāc epistulā Agricola victōriam Rōmānōrum Imperātōrī nūntiat.

1 'exercitus Rōmānus Calēdoniōs superāvit!'

Agricola dīcit exercitum Rōmānum Calēdoniōs superāvisse.

2 'multī hostēs periērunt, paucī effūgērunt.'

Agricola dīcit multōs hostēs periisse, paucōs effūgisse.

3 'aliae gentēs nūntiōs iam mīsērunt quī pācem petant.'

Agricola dīcit aliās gentēs nūntiōs mīsisse quī pācem petant.

epistula

Cn. Iūlius Agricola Domitiānō Imperātōrī salūtem dīcit.
septimus annus est, domine, ex quō pater tuus, dīvus
Vespasiānus, ad prōvinciam Britanniam mē mīsit, ut barbarōs
superārem. tū ipse, audītīs precibus meīs, iussistī Calēdoniōs
quoque in populī Rōmānī potestātem redigī. nunc tibi nūntiō   5
exercitum Rōmānum magnam victōriam rettulisse. bellum est
cōnfectum; Calēdoniī sunt victī.

    initiō huius aestātis, exercitus noster ad ultimās partēs
Britanniae pervēnit. hostēs, adventū nostrō cognitō, prope
montem Graupium sē ad proelium īnstrūxērunt. ibi mīlitēs   10
nostrī, spē glōriae adductī, victōriam nōmine tuō dignam
rettulērunt. incertum est quot hostēs perierint; sciō tamen
paucissimōs effūgisse. explōrātōrēs meī affirmant nōnnūllōs
superstitēs, salūte dēspērātā, etiam casās suās incendisse atque
uxōrēs līberōsque manū suā occīdisse.   15

    dē bellō satis dīxī. nunc pāx firmanda est. ego ipse Britannōs
hortātus sum ut templa, fora, domōs exstruant; fīliīs prīncipum
persuāsī ut linguam Latīnam discant. mōrēs Rōmānī ā Britannīs
iam adsūmuntur; ubīque geruntur togae.

    ūna cūra tamen mē sollicitat. timeō nē inquiēta sit Britannia,   20
dum Hibernia īnsula in lībertāte manet. quod sī Hibernōs
superāverimus, nōn modo pācem in Britanniā habēbimus, sed
etiam magnās dīvitiās comparābimus; audiō enim ex
mercātōribus metalla Hiberniae aurum multum continēre.
equidem crēdō hanc īnsulam legiōne ūnā obtinērī posse. mīlitēs   25
sunt parātī; signum Imperātōris alacriter exspectātur. valē.

Cn. = Gnaeus

**in ... potestātem redigī: in
  potestātem redigere** *bring
  under the control*
**victōriam rettulisse: victōriam
  referre** *win a victory*
initiō: initium *beginning*
aestātis: aestās *summer*
proelium *battle*

firmanda est: firmāre
  strengthen, establish

adsūmuntur: adsūmere *adopt*
sollicitat: sollicitāre *worry*
timeō nē *I am afraid that*
inquiēta: inquiētus *unsettled*
Hibernia *Ireland*
quod sī *but if*
aurum *gold*
equidem *indeed*
obtinērī: obtinēre *hold*
alacriter *eagerly*

*Drawing of a coin (a brass sestertius) issued shortly after the battle of
Mons Graupius.*

amīcī prīncipis

When you have read this story, answer the questions on the next page.

diē illūcēscente, complūrēs senātōrēs in aulam Domitiānī conveniēbant. nam Domitiānus cōnsilium suum ad aulam arcessī iusserat. L. Catullus Messālīnus, vir maximae auctōritātis, et Q. Vibius Crispus, senātor septuāgintā annōs nātus, dum Imperātōrem exspectant, anxiī inter sē colloquēbantur.   5

Q. = Quīntus

Messālīnus:	cūr adeō perturbāris, mī Crispe? nōn intellegō quārē anxius sīs.
Crispus:	nōn sine causā perturbor. ego enim prīmus ā Domitiānō sententiam rogābor, quia cōnsulāris sum nātū maximus. at nisi sciam quārē Domitiānus nōs arcessīverit, sententiam bene meditātam prōpōnere nōn poterō.
Messālīnus:	difficile est mihi tē adiuvāre, mī amīce. nescio enim quārē Domitiānus nōs cōnsulere velit. aliī dīcunt nūntium ē Britanniā advēnisse; aliī putant Germānōs rebellāvisse; aliī crēdunt ministrōs Epaphrodītī coniūrātiōnem dēprehendisse. nōn tamen tibi timendum est; tū enim es senātor summae auctōritātis.
Crispus:	id quod dīcis fortasse vērum est. nihilōminus mihi semper difficile est intellegere quāle respōnsum Domitiānus cupiat. sēnsūs enim vērōs dissimulāre solet. sī tamen tū mē adiūveris, sēcūrus erō. vīsne, quicquid dīxerō, sententiam similem prōpōnere?
Messālīnus:	minimē! perīculum mihi ipsī facere haudquāquam volō. nihil dīcam priusquam Epaphrodītī sententiam audīverō.
Crispus:	sed –
Messālīnus:	tacē, mī amīce! adest Imperātor.

Line numbers: 10, 15, 20, 25, 30

cōnsulāris *ex-consul*

meditātam: meditārī *consider*

putant: putāre *think*
ministrōs: minister *servant, agent*
dēprehendisse: dēprehendere *discover*

sēnsūs: sēnsus *feeling*
quicquid *whatever*
similem: similis *similar*

Questions

1   At what time of day did this conversation take place?   1
2   Why were the senators gathering in the palace?   2
3   Which Latin word shows how Messalinus and Crispus were feeling (lines 3–6)?   1
4   **ego enim … maximus** (lines 9–11). Who will be asked for an opinion first? Why?   2
5   What does he need to know before he can give a well-considered opinion (lines 11–13)?   1
6   Messalinus mentions three rumours he has heard (lines 15–18). What are they?   3
7   **nōn tamen … auctōritātis** (lines 18–20). How does Messalinus try to reassure Crispus?   2
8   What favour does Crispus ask from Messalinus (lines 24–5)?   2
9   Why does Messalinus refuse (lines 26–7)?   2
10 What impression do you get in this passage of
   a Domitian
   b Epaphroditus?
   Make one point about each character and support your answer by referring to the text.   2 + 2

TOTAL **20**

About the language 1: indirect statement (perfect active infinitive)

1   Compare the following direct and indirect statements:

<table>
<tr><td>

direct statements
'servus fūgit.'
'The slave has fled.'

</td><td>

indirect statements
dominus crēdit servum **fūgisse**.
The master believes the slave to have fled.
Or, in more natural English:
The master believes that the slave has fled.

</td></tr>
<tr><td>

'Rōmānī multa oppida dēlēvērunt.'
'The Romans have destroyed many towns.'

</td><td>

audiō Rōmānōs multa oppida **dēlēvisse**.
I hear that the Romans have destroyed many towns.

</td></tr>
</table>

The form of the verb in **bold type** is known as the perfect active infinitive.

2   Further examples:

a   'hostēs castra in rīpā flūminis posuērunt.'
b   centuriō dīcit hostēs castra in rīpā flūminis posuisse.
c   'Rōmānī magnam victōriam rettulērunt.'
d   in hāc epistulā Agricola nūntiat Rōmānōs magnam victōriam rettulisse.
e   clientēs putant patrōnum ex urbe discessisse.
f   sciō senātōrem vīllam splendidam in Campāniā aedificāvisse.

3   Compare the perfect active infinitive with the perfect active indicative:

perfect active indicative (1st person singular)		*perfect active infinitive*	
portāvī	*I have carried*	portāvisse	*to have carried*
docuī	*I have taught*	docuisse	*to have taught*
trāxī	*I have dragged*	trāxisse	*to have dragged*
audīvī	*I have heard*	audīvisse	*to have heard*

cōnsilium Domitiānī

I

dum senātōrēs anxiī inter sē colloquuntur, ingressus est
Domitiānus vultū ita compositō ut nēmō intellegere posset
utrum īrātus an laetus esset. eum sequēbātur Epaphrodītus,
epistulam manū tenēns.

Domitiānus, ā senātōribus salūtātus, 'nūntius', inquit, 'nōbīs   5
epistulam modo attulit, ā Cn. Iūliō Agricolā missam. in hāc

epistulā Agricola nūntiat exercitum
Rōmānum ad ultimās partēs
Britanniae pervēnisse et magnam
victōriam rettulisse. affirmat bellum   10
cōnfectum esse. Epaphrodīte,
epistulam recitā.'

epistulā recitātā, Domitiānus, ad
Crispum statim conversus,
'quid', inquit, 'dē hāc Agricolae   15
epistulā putās? quid mihi suādēs?'

Crispus diū tacēbat; superciliīs
contractīs quasi rem cōgitāret, oculōs
humī dēfīxit. dēnique:
'moderātiōnem', inquit, 'suādeō.'   20
Domitiānus 'breviter', inquit, 'et prūdenter locūtus es. tua
tamen sententia amplius est explicanda.'

priusquam Crispus respondēret, A. Fabricius Vēientō, cēterīs
paulō audācior, interpellāvit. veritus tamen nē Domitiānum

offenderet, verbīs cōnsīderātīs ūsus   25
est:

'cognōvimus, domine, Calēdoniōs
tandem victōs esse. Agricola tamen
hāc victōriā nimis ēlātus est. nam
crēdit īnsulam Hiberniam facile   30
occupārī posse; ego autem putō
Agricolam longē errāre; Hibernī enim
et ferōcēs et validī sunt. sī cōpiae
nostrae trāns mare in Hiberniam
ductae erunt, magnō perīculō   35
obicientur. revocandus est Agricola.'

quibus verbīs offēnsus, M'. Acīlius
Glabriō, 'equidem valdē gaudeō', inquit, 'Calēdoniōs superātōs
esse. sī Hibernia quoque ab Agricolā victa erit, tōtam Britanniam
in potestāte nostrā habēbimus. absurdum est Agricolam   40
revocāre priusquam Britannōs omnīnō superet! quis nostrōrum
ducum est melior quam Agricola? quis dignior est triumphō?'

---

modo *just now*
suādēs: suādēre *advise,*
suggest
superciliīs contractīs:
supercilia contrahere *draw*
eyebrows together, frown
moderātiōnem: moderātiō
moderation, caution
breviter *briefly*
prūdenter *prudently, sensibly*
amplius *more fully*
A. = Aulus
veritus: verērī *be afraid, fear*
cōnsīderātīs: cōnsīderātus
careful, well-considered
ūsus est: ūtī *use*
ēlātus *excited, carried away*
cōpiae *forces*
obicientur: obicere *put in the*
way of, expose to

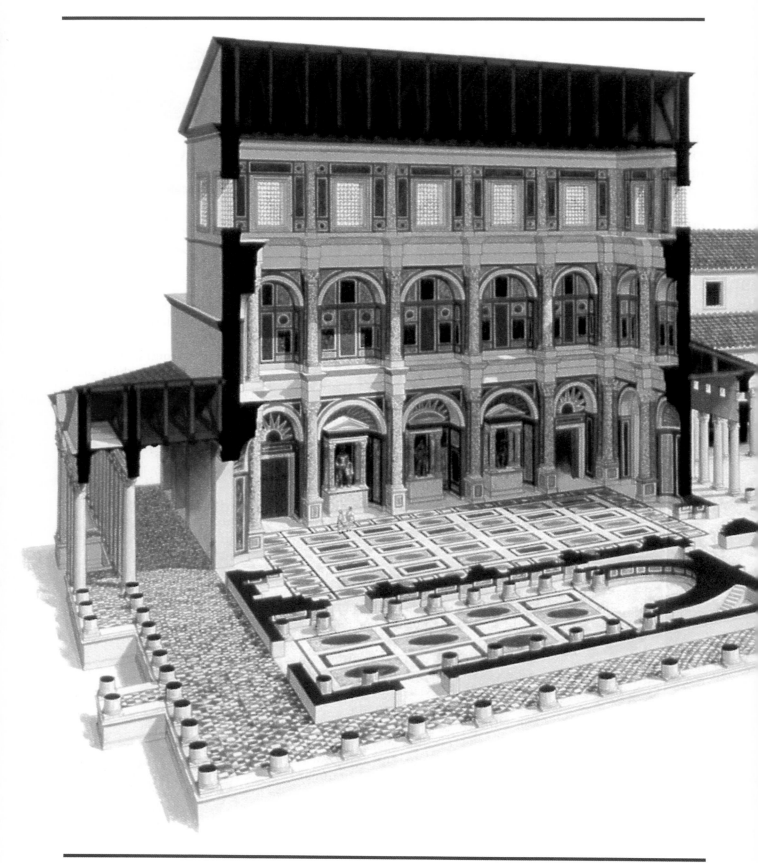

Above: *A reconstruction of part of Domitian's enormous palace on the Palatine Hill. At the left there is a large hall (aula) where the emperor's consilium might have met. It was flanked by two other large rooms. In the centre is a peristylium with a fountain, and on the right, a vast dining-room.*

Right: *The remains of the porch in front of the large hall (at the left in the reconstruction). Built of brick-faced concrete, the palace was covered in coloured marbles.*

II

cēterī, audāciā Glabriōnis obstupefactī, oculōs in
Imperātōrem dēfīxōs tenēbant nec quicquam dīcere audēbant.
ille tamen nec verbō nec vultū sēnsūs ostendit. deinde
Epaphrodītus, ad Glabriōnem
conversus,   5
'num comparās', inquit, 'hanc
inānem Agricolae victōriam cum
rēbus splendidīs ab Imperātōre
nostrō gestīs? nōnne audīvistī, mī
Glabriō, Imperātōrem ipsum   10
proximō annō multa mīlia
Germānōrum superāvisse? num
oblītus es prīncipēs Germānōs,
catēnīs vīnctōs, per viās urbis in
triumphō dēductōs esse?'   15
tum Messālīnus, simulatque haec
Epaphrodītī verba audīvit, occāsiōne
ūsus,
'scīmus', inquit, 'nūllōs hostēs ferōciōrēs Germānīs esse,
nūllum ducem Domitiānō Augustō esse meliōrem. scīmus etiam   20
Agricolam in prōvinciā septem
annōs mānsisse. ipse affirmat tam
fidēlēs sibi legiōnēs esse ut ad
Hiberniam sine timōre prōgredī
possit. cavendum est nōbīs! timeō nē 25
Agricola, spē imperiī adductus, in
Ītaliam cum legiōnibus reveniat
bellumque contrā patriam gerat.
num Glabriō cupit Agricolam fierī
Imperātōrem? Agricola, meā   30
sententiā, revocandus, laudandus,
tollendus est.'
Glabriō nihil respondit. nōn enim
dubitābat quīn Imperātōrem
graviter offendisset. Messālīnī sententiam cēterī senātōrēs   35
alacriter secūtī sunt.
Domitiānus autem nūllum signum dedit neque odiī neque
gaudiī neque invidiae. cōnsiliō tandem dīmissō, in ātriō sōlus
mānsit; multa in animō dē Glabriōne atque Agricolā volvēbat.

comparās: comparāre *compare*

gestīs: gerere *achieve*

proximō: proximus *last*

oblītus es: oblīvīscī *forget*

imperiī: imperium *power*

fierī *to become, to be made*

tollendus: tollere *remove, do away with*

nōn ... dubitābat quīn *did not doubt that*

invidiae: invidia *jealousy, envy*

About the language 2: indirect statement (perfect passive infinitive)

1   Compare the following direct and indirect statements:

> *direct statements*　　　　　　　　　*indirect statements*
> 'captīvī līberātī sunt.'　　　　　scio captīvōs **līberātōs esse**.
> *The prisoners have been freed.'*　*I know the prisoners to have been freed.*
> 　　　　　　　　　　　　　　Or, in more natural English:
> 　　　　　　　　　　　　　　*I know that the prisoners have been freed.*
>
> 'nūntius ab Agricolā missus est.'　lībertus dīcit nūntium ab Agricolā
> 　　　　　　　　　　　　　　**missum esse**.
> *'A messenger has been sent by*　　*The freedman says that a messenger has*
> *Agricola.'*　　　　　　　　　　*been sent by Agricola.*

The form of the verb in **bold type** is known as the perfect passive infinitive.

2   Further examples:

   a   'multī Calēdoniī occīsī sunt.'
   b   in hāc epistulā Agricola nūntiat multōs Calēdoniōs occīsōs esse.
   c   'templum novum in forō exstrūctum est.'
   d   mercātōrēs dīcunt templum novum in forō exstrūctum esse.
   e   audiō lībertātem omnibus servīs datam esse.
   f   nauta crēdit quattuor nāvēs tempestāte dēlētās esse.

3   Compare the perfect passive indicative and the perfect passive infinitive:

perfect passive indicative (1st person singular)		*perfect passive infinitive*	
portātus sum	*I have been carried*	portātus esse	*to have been carried*
doctus sum	*I have been taught*	doctus esse	*to have been taught*
tractus sum	*I have been dragged*	tractus esse	*to have been dragged*
audītus sum	*I have been heard*	audītus esse	*to have been heard*

Notice that the perfect passive infinitive contains the perfect passive participle (**portātus**, etc.) which changes its ending in the usual way to agree with the noun it describes:

> videō cibum **parātum** esse.　　　videō nāvēs **parātās** esse.
> *I see that the food has been prepared.*　*I see that the ships have been prepared.*

Word patterns: verbs and nouns

1   Study the form and meaning of the following verbs and nouns:

ōrnāre	*to decorate*	ōrnāmentum	*decoration*
impedīre	*to hinder*	impedīmentum	*hindrance, nuisance*
nōmināre	*to nominate, name*	nōmen	*name*
volvere	*to turn, roll*	volūmen	*roll of papyrus, scroll*

2   Now complete the following table:

torquēre	*to torture, twist*	tormentum	. . . .
arguere	. . . .	argūmentum	*proof, argument*
vestīre	*to clothe, dress*	vestīmenta	. . . .
certāre	*to compete*	certāmen	. . . .
crīmināre	*to accuse*	crīmen	. . . .
fluere	. . . .	flūmen	. . . .

3   Match each of the following Latin nouns with the correct English translation:

> Latin: blandīmentum, incitāmentum, cōnāmen, mūnīmentum, sōlāmen.
> English: effort, flattery, encouragement, comfort, defence.

4   What is the gender of these nouns? How do they decline? If necessary,
    see pp. 104–5.

Practising the language

1   Complete each sentence with the most suitable word from the box below, and
    then translate.

> audītō   aedificābātur   poterant   prōcēdere   Imperātōrī   esset

a   in summō monte novum templum . . . .
b   nūntius, simulatque advēnit, ... epistulam trādidit.
c   strepitū . . . ., cōnsul ē lectō surrēxit.
d   facile cognōvī quis auctor pugnae . . . .
e   puto pompam per forum iam . . . .
f   post proelium paucī Calēdoniī effugere . . . .

2 Translate the first sentence of each pair. Then, with the help of p. 116, complete the second sentence with a passive form of the verb to express the same idea. Finally, translate the second sentence.

For example: senātōrēs Domitiānum timent.
Domitiānus ā senātōribus timē… .
Translated and completed, this becomes:
senātōrēs Domitiānum timent.
The senators fear Domitian.
Domitiānus ā senātōribus timētur.
Domitian is feared by the senators.

a dux equitēs iam incitat.
equitēs ā duce iam incita… .
b exercitus noster oppidum mox dēlēbit.
oppidum ab exercitū nostrō mox dēlē… .

In sentences **c–f**, nouns as well as verbs have to be completed. Refer if necessary to the table of nouns on pp. 104–5.

c multī cīvēs lūdōs spectābunt.
lūdī ā multīs cīv… spectā… .
d puellae ātrium ōrnant.
ātrium ā puell… ōrnā… .
e puer victimās ad āram dūcēbat.
victimae ad āram ā puer… dūcē… .
f mercātor servum accūsābit.
serv… ā mercātōr… accūsā… .

3 Translate each sentence into Latin by selecting correctly from the list of Latin words.

a *The barbarians have been surrounded by our army.*

| barbarī | ad exercitum | nostrō | circumventus est |
| barbarīs | ab exercitū | noster | circumventī sunt |

b *A certain senator is trying to deceive you.*

| senātōrī | quīdam | tē | dēcipit | cōnātur |
| senātor | quidem | tuī | dēcipere | cōnantur |

c *He was lying hidden, in order to hear the old men's conversation.*

| latēbat | ut | sermōnem | senem | audīvisset |
| latuerat | nē | sermō | senum | audīret |

d *The same clients will be here tomorrow.*

| eōsdem | cliēns | crās | aderunt |
| eīdem | clientēs | cotīdiē | aberunt |

e *The originator of the crime did not want to be seen in the forum.*

| auctor | scelerī | in forum | vidēre | volēbat |
| auctōrem | sceleris | in forō | vidērī | nōlēbat |

The emperor's council

Among the people who took part in the government of the empire were the members of the emperor's **cōnsilium** (council), often referred to as **amīcī** (friends) of the emperor.

The consilium did not have a fixed membership; it was simply made up of those people whom the emperor invited to advise him on any particular occasion. Some men were regularly asked to meetings of the consilium; others were asked occasionally. Many would be experienced and distinguished men of senatorial rank, who had reached the top of the career ladder described on pp. 45–7. Some men of equestrian rank might also be invited, such as the commander of the praetorian guard. When there was a change of emperor, the new emperor usually invited some new members to meetings of the consilium, but also found it convenient to continue using some of the previous emperor's advisers. In many cases the new emperor had himself attended the previous emperor's consilium.

The matters on which the emperor asked his consilium for advice were naturally varied. The consilium might, for example, be summoned in moments of crisis, such as the discovery of a conspiracy against the emperor's life; or it might be consulted on the delicate question: 'Who should be the emperor's heir?' Sometimes the emperor would want advice about military decisions or foreign affairs. The story on pp. 37 and 40, in which Domitian asks his advisers about Agricola's letter from Britain, is fictitious, but it would not have been odd or unusual for the consilium to have discussed such a question.

Relief showing an emperor dealing with affairs of state, seated on a platform in front of the Basilica Julia in the Forum.

However, the commonest task of the amici was to advise the emperor while he was administering the law. For example, they might join him when he was hearing an appeal by a condemned prisoner, or settling a property dispute between two or more parties. After the people concerned had stated their case, the emperor would ask for the **sententia** (opinion) of each member of the consilium in turn; he might then retire for further thought, and would finally announce his decision. He was not bound to follow the majority opinion of the consilium, and could even ignore their advice altogether. In theory, the amici were free to give their opinions firmly and frankly; but under some emperors it could be dangerous to speak one's mind too openly.

Some of the cases which were heard by the Emperor Trajan are described by Pliny, who was sometimes invited to Trajan's consilium. They include a charge of adultery against a military tribune's wife and a centurion, and a dispute in a small town in Gaul where the local mayor had abolished the town's annual games. It is clear from Pliny's account that even quite trivial cases were sometimes referred to the emperor for decision; most Roman emperors were kept very busy, and needed the help of their amici in order to cope with the workload.

The senatorial career

Most of the amici taking part in the discussion on pp. 37 and 40 would have successfully followed a career known as the senatorial **cursus honōrum** (series of honours or ladder of promotion) in which members of the senatorial class competed with each other for official posts in the Roman government. These official posts were arranged in a fixed order, and as a man worked his way through them, his responsibilities and status steadily increased. Some posts were compulsory, so that a man who had not held a particular post was not allowed to proceed to a higher one, except by special favour of the emperor. The most successful men got to the top, and the rest dropped out at various points along the way.

Some officials, such as the consuls, were chosen by the emperor; others were elected by the senate. Even in those posts where the choice was made by the senate, the emperor still had great influence, since he could 'recommend' to the senate particular candidates for election.

By the time of Domitian, the most important stages in the cursus honorum were as follows:

Holders of the senior posts – aediles, praetors and consuls – had the honour of sitting in an ivory-inlaid 'curule chair'.

The senatorial cursus honorum

1 vīgintīvir. Every year twenty young men were chosen as vigintiviri, who served for a year in Rome as junior officials, assisting with such tasks as the management of the law courts and prisons, and the minting of the Roman coinage.

2 tribūnus mīlitum. In the following year, each of the young men went abroad on military service as an officer in a legion.

3 quaestor. On returning to Rome, a man who wanted to progress further in the cursus honorum would aim at the quaestorship. This post involved the management of sums of public money and was usually (but not always) held in Rome. It lasted for one year and was important because it qualified a man for entry into the senate, which met regularly to discuss and decide government business.

4 tribūnus plēbis or **aedīlis**. After a compulsory interval of a year, an ex-quaestor who wanted further promotion had a choice. He might aim to become one of the ten tribunes of the people, whose original responsibility had been to act as helpers and advisers of the common people (**plēbs**), but whose tasks had been greatly reduced by the time of Domitian. Alternatively, he could try to be appointed as one of the six aediles, who were responsible for the upkeep of public buildings, baths, sewers and roads.

5 praetor. The chief task of the praetors was to supervise the Roman law courts. A man who had held the praetorship also became eligible for certain important posts abroad; for example, he might command a legion, or govern one of the twenty-eight provinces (but not the ten most important ones). Governorships of provinces were normally held for a period of three years.

6 cōnsul. The highest post in the cursus honorum was the consulship. There were only two consuls at any one time, but they changed at intervals during the year. They presided at meetings of the senate, and had a general responsibility for supervising government business. The ablest ex-consuls became governors of the ten most important provinces; some men, through exceptional ability or by favour of the emperor, achieved further distinctions, including second or even third consulships.

C PLINIO L F
OVF CAECILIO
SECVNDO COS
AVGVR CVR ALV TIB
ET RIP ET CLOAC VRB
PRAEF AER SAT
PRAEF
AER MIL Q IMP
SEVIR EQ R TR MIL
LEG III GALL XVIRO
STL IVD FL DIVI T AVG
VERCELLENSES

Above: *An inscription, with transcript, setting out the career of Pliny, found in a town where he had a villa. It was set up in his honour by the people of Vercellae. His final posting, to Bithynia, must have come later (coin of Nicaea in Bithynia, below).*

This system enabled the emperor to see who the ablest men were. It also showed him whether a man had any special skills which made him suitable for a particular job or province. For example, Agricola was a good soldier, while Pliny was an expert in financial matters; each man was given work that offered him opportunities to use his particular gifts. The careers of both men are given below. They differ from each other in the early stages, because Agricola did not become a vigintivir and had an unusually long period as a military tribune. Pliny's career looks somewhat fuller than Agricola's; this is partly because Agricola's governorship of Britain was exceptionally lengthy, and partly because Agricola held no post at all between his recall from Britain and his death.

Career of Agricola		Career of Pliny	
AD		AD	
40	birth	61 or 62	birth
		?82	vigintivir (with responsibility for one of the law courts)
58–61	tribunus militum in Britain	?83	tribunus militum in Syria
64	quaestor in Asia	90	quaestor in Rome
66	tribunus plebis	92	tribunus plebis
68	praetor	93	praetor
70–73	legatus legionis XX in Britain	94–96	praefectus aerarii militaris (in charge of the military treasury)
74–76	legatus (governor) of Aquitania	98–100	praefectus aerarii Saturni (in charge of the state treasury in the temple of Saturn)
77	consul	100	consul
78–84	legatus (governor) of Britain	103	augur (honorary priesthood, held simultaneously with other posts)
		104–106	curator Tiberis (responsible for flood precautions, drainage, etc., in connection with river Tiber)
		109–111	legatus Augusti in Bithynia (a special governorship by personal appointment of the emperor)
93	death	111	death

Several of the above dates, especially in the early part of Pliny's career, are approximate and uncertain.

Vocabulary checklist 37

complūrēs, complūra	several
dignus, digna, dignum	worthy, appropriate
discō, discere, didicī	learn
dīvus, dīvī	god
dubitō, dubitāre, dubitāvī	hesitate, doubt
exercitus, exercitūs	army
fīō, fierī, factus sum	become, be made
oblīvīscor, oblīvīscī, oblītus sum	forget
odium, odiī	hatred
patria, patriae	country, homeland
paulō	a little
perturbō, perturbāre, perturbāvī, perturbātus	alarm, disturb
proelium, proeliī	battle
puto, putāre, putāvī	think
revocō, revocāre, revocāvī, revocātus	recall, call back
sēcūrus, sēcūra, sēcūrum	without a care
tempestās, tempestātis	storm
trāns	across
validus, valida, validum	strong

Pliny's experience as Prefect of the Treasury of Saturn (housed in this temple overlooking the Forum Romanum) prepared him for sorting out the considerable financial problems of Bithynia.

NUPTIAE

STAGE 38

Imperātōris sententia

When you have read this story, answer the questions on the next page.

in aulā Domitiānī, T. Flāvius Clēmēns, adfīnis Imperātōris, cum Domitiānō anxius colloquitur. Clēmēns semper cum Imperātōre cōnsentīre solet; verētur enim nē idem sibi accidat ac frātrī, quī iussū Imperātōris occīsus est.

Domitiānus:	decōrum est mihi, mī Clēmēns, tē līberōsque tuōs honōrāre. ego ipse, ut scīs, līberōs nūllōs habeō quī imperium post mortem meam exerceant. cōnstituī igitur fīliōs tuōs in familiam meam ascīscere. cognōmina 'Domitiānum' et 'Vespasiānum' eīs dabō; praetereā rhētorem nōtissimum eīs praeficiam, M. Fabium Quīntiliānum. prō certō habeō Quīntiliānum eōs optimē doctūrum esse.	5
		10
Clēmēns:	grātiās maximās tibi agō, domine, quod mē fīliōsque meōs tantō honōre afficis. ego semper –	15
Domitiānus:	satis! pauca nunc dē Pōllā, fīliā tuā, loquī velim. crēdō Pōllam quattuordecim annōs iam nātam esse. nōnne necesse est nōbīs eam in mātrimōnium collocāre?	
Clēmēns:	domine –	20
Domitiānus:	virum quendam cognōvī quī omnī modō fīliā tuā dignus est. commendō tibi Sparsum, senātōrem summae virtūtis quī magnās dīvitiās possidet.	
Clēmēns:	at, domine, iam quīnquāgintā annōs nātus est Sparsus.	25
Domitiānus:	ita vērō! aetāte flōret.	
Clēmēns:	at bis mātrimōniō iūnctus, utramque uxōrem repudiāvit.	
Domitiānus:	prō certō habeō eum numquam cognātam Imperātōris repudiātūrum esse. quid multa? prōmittō Sparsum tibi generum grātissimum futūrum esse. haec est sententia mea, quam sī dissēnseris mūtābō. sed prius tibi explicandum erit quārē dissentiās.	30

---

adfīnis *relative, relation by marriage*
idem ... ac *the same ... as*

ascīscere *adopt*
cognōmina: cognōmen *surname, additional name*

afficis: afficere *treat*

quattuordecim *fourteen*

virtūtis: virtūs *virtue*
aetāte flōret: aetāte flōrēre *be in the prime of life*
bis *twice*
iūnctus: iungere *join*
utramque: uterque *each, both*
repudiāvit: repudiāre *divorce*
cognātam: cognāta *relative (by birth)*
quid multa? *what more is there to say?, in short*
generum: gener *son-in-law*
grātissimum: grātus *acceptable, pleasing*
mūtābō: mūtāre *change*

prō certō habeō
Quīntiliānum eōs optimē
doctūrum esse.

Questions

Marks

1 What is taking place in the palace?   1

2 What attitude does Clemens always take towards Domitian? Why?   1 + 3

3 What is Domitian proposing to do (lines 5–6)?   1

4 What problem does he have (lines 6–7)?   2

5 How has he decided to solve it (lines 8–9)?   1

6 What arrangements will he make about the boys' education? What guarantee does he make to Clemens (lines 10–13)?   2

7 What proposal does Domitian make about Polla? Why does he think it is the right time to make it?   2

8 **commendō … possidet** (lines 22–3). Why does Domitian recommend Sparsus?   2

9 What is the first objection Clemens makes to Sparsus (lines 24–5)? What do you think of Domitian's reply?   2

10 What is Clemens' second objection (lines 27–8)? Do you think Domitian's answer is convincing (lines 29–30)? Give a reason.   2 + 1

11 **haec est … dissentiās** (lines 32–4). What does Domitian say he will do if Clemens disagrees? What condition does he attach? Do you think Clemens will disagree? Give a reason.   3

12 What does this story tell us about Domitian's attitude to his family? Make two points.   2

TOTAL   **25**

Pōlla

Pōlla, fīlia Clēmentis, fortūnam suam queritur; māter Flāvia eam cōnsōlārī cōnātur.

Pōlla: quam crūdēlis est pater meus, quī mē Sparsō nūbere iussit! quid faciam, māter? num putās mē istī senī umquam nūptūram esse? scīs mē alium quendam amāre.
                   5

Flāvia: ō dēliciae, nōlī lacrimāre! dūra est vīta; necesse est pārēre eīs quī nōs regunt. crēdō tamen Sparsum satis grātum et benignum tibi futūrum esse.

Pōlla: cūr mē ita dēcipis? scīs eum esse senem odiōsum. scīs etiam eum duās uxōrēs iam repudiāvisse. at tū, māter, sententiā Imperātōris nimis movēris; nihil dē mē cūrās, nihil dē Helvidiō quem amō.
                10

Flāvia: num tū tam audāx es ut istī amōrī indulgeās? iste enim Helvidius gentī nostrae est odiō. num oblīta es avum eius, cum Vespasiānum Imperātōrem graviter offendisset, in exiliō occīsum esse? mihi crēde, mea Pōlla! melius est cēdere quam frūstrā resistere.
                15

queritur: querī *lament, complain about*
cōnsōlārī *console*
nūbere *marry*
quid faciam? *what am I to do?*

odiōsum: odiōsus *hateful*

movēris: movēre *move, influence*
indulgeās: indulgēre *give way to*
avum: avus *grandfather*
exiliō: exilium *exile*

Sculptures of Roman married couples often show that the man was older than the woman.

About the language 1: indirect statement (future active infinitive)

1 Compare the following direct and indirect statements:

direct statements
'hostēs mox pugnābunt.'
'The enemy will fight soon.'

indirect statements
crēdimus hostēs mox **pugnātūrōs esse**.
We believe the enemy to be going to fight soon.
Or, in more natural English:
We believe that the enemy will fight soon.

'senex perībit.'
'The old man will die.'

medicus dīcit senem **peritūrum esse**.
The doctor says that the old man will die.

The form of the verb in **bold type** is known as the future active infinitive.

2 Further examples:

a 'multī āthlētae crās certābunt.'
b praecō dīcit multōs āthlētās crās certātūrōs esse.
c 'novae cōpiae mox advenient.'
d mīlitēs crēdunt novās cōpiās mox adventūrās esse.
e suspicor ancillam tē dēceptūram esse.
f mercātor spērat sē magnās dīvitiās comparātūrum esse.

3 Study the way in which the future active infinitive is formed:

portātūrus esse
to be about to carry

doctūrus esse
to be about to teach

tractūrus esse
to be about to drag

audītūrus esse
to be about to hear

Notice that the future active infinitive contains the future participle (**portātūrus**, etc.) which changes its ending in the usual way to agree with the noun it describes:

puer dīcit patrem crās **reventūrum** esse.
The boy says that his father will return tomorrow.

puer dīcit fēminās crās **reventūrās** esse.
The boy says that the women will return tomorrow.

prīdiē nūptiārum

prīdiē *the day before*

nox est. crās nūptiae Pōllae et Sparsī celebrābuntur. Pōlla per hortum patris errat. crēdit sē sōlam esse; ignōrat Helvidium advēnisse. quī, hortum clam ingressus, Pōllam querentem audit; inter arborēs immōtus stat.

errat: errāre *wander*

Pōlla:	quid faciam? Helvidius trēs diēs iam abest, neque scio quō ille ierit. intereā tōtam domum nostram videō ad nūptiās meās odiōsās parārī. ō Helvidī, ēripe mē ex hīs malīs!	5

ēripe: ēripere *rescue, snatch away*

Helvidius:	(*subitō prōgressus*) id libenter faciam. nēmō mē prohibēbit.	10
Pōlla:	(*gaudiō et pavōre commōta*) Helvidī! quō modō hūc vēnistī? sī hīc captus eris, interficiēris. fuge, priusquam pater meus tē cōnspiciat!	
Helvidius:	fugiam vērō, sed nōn sine tē. fuge mēcum, mea Pōlla! tē ex hīs malīs ēripiam, sīcut tū modo precābāris.	15
Pōlla:	quō modō fugere possumus? tū ipse scīs mē semper custōdīrī. nūptiās odiōsās nūllō modō vītāre possum. parentēs, Imperātor, lēgēs mē iubent cōguntque Sparsō nūbere.	20
Helvidius:	minimē, mea Pōlla! tibi polliceor mē moritūrum esse priusquam ille senex tē uxōrem dūcat. nōbīs procul ex hāc urbe fugiendum est, ubi parentēs tuī nōs invenīre numquam poterunt.	

uxōrem dūcat: uxōrem dūcere *take as a wife, marry*

Pōlla:	distrahor et excrucior. hūc amor, illūc pietās mē trahit.	25
Helvidius:	nōlī timēre, mea Pōlla! tē numquam dēseram, semper servābō.	
Flāvia:	(*intrā domum*) Pōlla! Pōlla, ubi es?	
Pōlla:	ēheu! ā mātre vocor. audī, mī Helvidī! haec ultima verba tibi dīcō; nōn enim putō mē umquam tē iterum vīsūram esse. crās ego Sparsō nūbam. est mihi nūlla spēs fugae. sed quamquam Sparsus mē uxōrem ductūrus est, mī Helvidī, iūrō mē tē sōlum amāre, iūrō mē … (*lacrimās retinēre frūstrā cōnātur*) tē semper amātūram … (*vōx dēficit*).	30
		35

distrahor: distrahere *tear apart, tear in two*
hūc … illūc *this way … that way, one way … another way*
pietās *duty*
intrā *inside*

iūrō: iūrāre *swear*
dēficit: dēficere *fail, die away*

Helvidius:	(*dextram Pōllae arripiēns*) Pōlla, deōs testor Sparsum tē uxōrem numquam ductūrum esse. cōnfīde mihi, mea Pōlla! (*Pōllam ardenter amplexus, Helvidius abit.*)	
Pōlla:	(*incerta utrum spēret an timeat*) dea Fortūna, servā eum!	40

dextram: dextra *right hand*
arripiēns: arripere *seize*
testor: testārī *call to witness*
ardenter *passionately*

About the language 2: perfect subjunctive

1   In Stage 36, you met the present subjunctive:

> incertus sum ubi Mārtiālis hodiē **recitet**.
> *I am not sure where Martial **is reciting** today.*

2   In Stages 37 and 38, you have met sentences like these:

> cognōscere volō quārē Domitiānus nōs **vocāverit**.
> *I want to find out why Domitian **has called** us.*

> senātor nescit quō modō Imperātōrem **offenderit**.
> *The senator does not know how he **has offended** the Emperor.*

The form of the verb in **bold type** is the perfect subjunctive.

3   Further examples:

  a   crās cognōscēmus quantam pecūniam parentēs nōbīs relīquerint.
  b   centuriō scīre vult num senex equum cōnspexerit.
  c   Pōlla nescit quō Helvidius ierit.
  d   uxor mē cotīdiē rogat quārē hanc vīllam ēmerim.
  e   incertī sumus utrum barbarī castra oppugnāverint an fūgerint.

4   Compare the perfect subjunctive with the perfect indicative:

perfect indicative	*perfect subjunctive*
portāvī	portāverim
portāvistī	portāverīs
portāvit	portāverit
portāvimus	portāverīmus
portāvistis	portāverītis
portāvērunt	portāverint

Perfect subjunctive forms of **doceō**, **trahō** and **audiō** are given on p. 118 of the Language Information section.

5   For the perfect subjunctive of irregular verbs, see p. 123.

cōnfarreātiō

cōnfarreātiō *wedding ceremony*

I

diēs nūptiārum adest. Pōlla, veste nūptiālī ōrnāta, in cubiculō suō stat. māter eam īnspicit.

veste: vestis *clothing, clothes*
nūptiālī: nūptiālis *wedding*

Flāvia:	nunc tē verte ad mē, Pōlla! flammeum firmē capitī superpositum est? (*Pōllam lacrimāre videt.*) ō mea fīlia, tibi haud lacrimandum est; diē nūptiārum nōn decōrum est lacrimāre.

flammeum *veil*
superpositum est:
  superpōnere *place on*

servus Clēmentis:	(*ingressus*) domina, iussus sum vōs ad sacrificium arcessere. dominus meus dīcit victimam iam ēlēctam esse, haruspicēs parātōs adstāre. nūntius quoque iam adest, quī dīcit Imperātōrem, comitante Sparsō, mox adventūrum esse.
Flāvia:	bene! nūntiā dominō tuō nōs statim ad ātrium prōcessūrās esse.

Flāvia et Pōlla ad ātrium prōcēdunt, ubi multī amīcī, familiārēs, clientēs iam adsunt. intrat Sparsus, multīs comitantibus servīs; deinde ingreditur ipse Domitiānus. Pōlla, valdē commōta, ad Sparsum dūcitur; dextrās sollemniter iungunt. inde Domitiānus, ut Pontifex Maximus, ad medium ātrium prōcēdit ut sacrificium Iovī faciat. victima ā Domitiānō sacrificātur; precēs Iovī et Iūnōnī offeruntur. Pōlla tamen adeō perturbātur ut precēs audīre vix possit.

Pontifex Maximus *Chief Priest*

Iūnōnī: Iūnō *Juno (goddess of marriage)*

Sparsus:	(*Pōllam perturbārī animadvertit.*) nōlī timēre, mea Pōlla! age! cōnsīde in hāc sellā. nunc cōnfarreātiōnem celebrābimus.
Domitiānus:	(*lībum farreum Sparsō et Pōllae offerēns*) hoc lībum sacrum cōnsūmite!

lībum farreum *cake made from grain*

Sparsus et Pōlla lībum sacrum cōnsūmunt.

Domitiānus:	tacēte vōs omnēs, quī adestis! vōbīs prōnūntiō hanc virginem nunc in manum huius virī convenīre.
spectātōrēs:	fēlīciter! fēlīciter!
Domitiānus:	nunc cēdite testibus! tabulae nūptiālēs signandae sunt.

in manum ... convenīre *pass into the hands of*
fēlīciter! *good luck!*
tabulae nūptiālēs *marriage contract, marriage tablets*

tabulīs signātīs, omnēs ad triclīnium prōcēdunt, ubi cēna sūmptuōsa parāta est.

Sparsus Pōllam perturbārī animadvertit.

II

sōle occidente, servī Pōllam domum Sparsī dēdūcere parant, ubi Sparsus, prior profectus, iam eam exspectat. chorus mūsicōrum carmen nūptiāle cantāre incipit.

chorus:	ō Hymēn Hymenaee, iō!
	ō Hymēn Hymenaee!
Flāvia:	mea fīlia, sīc tē amplexa valedīcō. valē, mea Pōlla, valē!

servī, ut mōs est, puellam ā mātre abripiunt. puerī, quī facēs ardentēs ferunt, Pōllam forās dēdūcunt. magnā comitante turbā pompa per viās prōgreditur.

chorus:	tollite, ō puerī, facēs!
	flammeum videō venīre.
	ō Hymēn Hymenaee, iō!
	ō Hymēn Hymenaee!

prior *earlier*
chorus *chorus, choir*
mūsicōrum: mūsicus *musician*
Hymēn *and* **Hymenaee:**
   Hymenaeus *Hymen (god of weddings)*

abripiunt: abripere *tear away from*
forās *out of the house*

III

*tandem pompa domum Sparsī, flōribus ōrnātam, advenit. quī, domō
ēgressus, Pōllam ita appellat:*

Sparsus:	siste! quis es tū? quō nōmine hūc venīs?
Pōlla:	ubi tū Gāius, ego Gāia.

*quibus verbīs sollemnibus dictīs, subitō magnus clāmor audītur; ē
mediā turbā ērumpit iuvenis, pugiōne armātus, quī praeceps in
Sparsum ruit.*

iuvenis:	nunc morere, Sparse! (*Sparsum ferōciter pugiōne petit.*)
Sparsus:	subvenīte! subvenīte!

*ingēns strepitus orītur; servī accurrunt; aliī spectātōrēs Sparsō
servīsque subveniunt, aliī immōtī et obstupefactī stant. Pōlla tamen,
iuvene Helvidiō agnitō, pallēscit. servī Helvidium, tandem
comprehēnsum, firmē retinent.*

siste: sistere *stop, halt*

5   **sollemnibus: sollemnis**
    solemn, traditional

morere! *die!*

10   **orītur: orīrī** *rise, arise*

Sparsus: (*exclāmāns*) illum agnōscō! Helvidius est, homō
īnfestissimus gentī Imperātōris. eum ad Imperātōrem   *15*
dūcite! prō certō habeō Domitiānum eī poenam
aptissimam excōgitātūrum esse. (*Pōlla horrēscit.*) nōlī
timēre, mea Pōlla! ille iuvenis īnsānus numquam
iterum nōs vexābit. nunc tibi tempus est domum
tuam novam intrāre.   *20*

excōgitātūrum esse:
   excōgitāre *invent, think up*
horrēscit: horrēscere *shudder*

*Sparsus Pōllam bracchiīs tollit ut eam trāns līmen portet. Helvidius ad
Domitiānum abdūcitur.*

About the language 3: indirect statement (present passive infinitive)

1   In Stage 34, you met the present passive infinitive, used in sentences like these:

>   **laudārī** volō.   sonitus **audīrī** nōn poterat.
>   *I want to be praised.*   *The sound was unable to be heard.*

2   In Stage 38, you have met the present passive infinitive in indirect statements.
Study the following examples:

>   *direct statements*   *indirect statements*
>   'vexāris.'   scio tē **vexārī**.
>   *'You are annoyed.'*   *I know you to be annoyed.*
>   Or, in more natural English:
>   *I know that you are annoyed.*
>
>   'multī mīlitēs exercentur.'   audīmus multōs mīlitēs **exercērī**.
>   *'Many soldiers are being trained.'*   *We hear that many soldiers are being trained.*

3   Further examples:

a   'cēna splendida in vīllā iam parātur.'
b   prō certō habeō cēnam splendidam in vīllā iam parārī.
c   'cōnsul morbō gravī afflīgitur.'
d   senātōrēs dīcunt cōnsulem morbō gravī afflīgī.
e   audiō filiōs Clēmentis ā Quīntiliānō cotīdiē docērī.
f   amīcus meus affirmat tē numquam ab Imperātōre laudārī, saepe culpārī.

4   The forms of the present passive infinitives are set out on p. 119.

amor et mātrimōnium

I *dē amīcō mūtābilī*

> difficilis facilis, iūcundus acerbus es īdem:
> nec tēcum possum vīvere nec sine tē.
> > *Martial*

How does Martial emphasise the contradictions in his friend's character and the effect they have on himself?

mūtābilī: mūtābilis *changeable, contradictory*
facilis *here = easy-going*
iūcundus *pleasant*
acerbus *harsh, disagreeable*
īdem *here = you, the same person*

II *dē Chloē, quae septem marītīs nūpsit*

> īnscrīpsit tumulīs septem scelerāta virōrum
> 'sē fēcisse' Chloē. quid pote simplicius?
> > *Martial*

What does Chloe mean by **sē fēcisse**? What meaning does Martial suggest?

The following lines are taken from a longer poem, possibly written by Petronius, Nero's **arbiter ēlegantiae** (adviser on good taste).

tumulīs: tumulus *tomb*
scelerāta: scelerātus *wicked*
virōrum: vir *here = husband*
quid pote? *what could be?*
simplicius: simplex *simple*

III *dē Cupīdine, deō potentī*

> ecce tacent vōcēs hominum strepitusque viārum
> et volucrum cantūs turbaque fīda canum:
> sōlus ego ex cūnctīs paveō somnumque torumque
> et sequor imperium, magne Cupīdo, tuum.

What contrasts do you find between the first two and the last two lines? What impression are you given of the god Cupid?

volucrum: volucris *bird*
cantūs: cantus *song*
fīda: fīdus *faithful*
cūnctīs: cūnctus *all*
paveō: pavēre *dread, fear*
somnum: somnus *sleep*
-que ... -que *both ... and*
torum: torus *bed*
imperium *here = command*

The Romans often decorated their walls, floors and (as here) their crockery with pictures of lovers.

Practising the language

1 Complete each sentence with the correct verb. Then translate the sentence.

    a cognōscere volō ubi fīlius vester . . . . (habitet, habitent)
    b tot gemmās ēmistī ut nūllam pecūniam iam . . . . (habeās, habeātis)
    c strēnuē labōrāmus ut opus ante lūcem . . . . (perficiam, perficiāmus)
    d tam fessus est amīcus meus ut longius prōgredī nōn . . . . (possit, possint)
    e senex nescit quārē puerī in viā . . . . (clāmēs, clāmet, clāment)
    f iterum vōs rogō num hunc virum . . . . (agnōscam, agnōscās, agnōscātis)

2 Translate the first sentence. Then change it from a direct statement to an indirect statement by completing the second sentence. Finally, translate the second sentence.

    For example:
        puer labōrat.   dominus putat puerum labōr… .
    Translated and completed, this becomes:
        puer labōrat.   dominus putat puerum labōrāre.
        The boy is working.   *The master thinks that the boy is working.*

    a multae vīllae ardent!
        senex dīcit multās vīllās ard… .
    b centuriō appropinquat.
        mīlitēs putant centuriōnem appropinqu… .
    c medicus tēcum cōnsentit.
        crēdō medicum tēcum cōnsent… .

    In sentences **d–f**, nouns as well as verbs have to be completed. Refer if necessary to the table of nouns on pp. 104–5.

    d rēx in illā aulā habitat.
        sciō rēg… in illā aulā habit… .
    e servī iam dormiunt.
        fūr crēdit serv… iam dorm… .
    f puella dentēs nigrōs habet.
        Mārtiālis dīcit puell… dentēs nigrōs hab… .

Marriage

The average age for a Roman girl to marry was about thirteen or fourteen; men usually married in their late teens or early twenties. If the husband had been married previously, like Sparsus in the story on p. 50, there might be a wide age gap between him and his wife.

The husband was normally chosen for the girl by her father or guardian. The law laid down that if the girl did not agree to the marriage, it could not take place; but probably few daughters would have found it very easy to defy their father's wishes. The girl's father would also negotiate with the family of her future husband about the **dōs** (dowry); this was a payment (in money or property or both) made by the bride's family to the husband.

At the ceremony of betrothal or engagement (**spōnsālia**), the husband-to-be made a promise of marriage, and the father of the bride promised on his daughter's behalf; gifts were exchanged, and a ring was placed on the third finger of the girl's left hand, as in many countries nowadays. (There was a widespread belief that a nerve ran directly from this finger to the heart.) Family and friends were present as witnesses, and the ceremony was followed by a party.

Above: Gold betrothal ring.

Below: Traditionally, girls were supposed to be unwilling to leave the safety of their parents' home for marriage. This painting shows a veiled bride, seated on the marriage bed, being coaxed by the goddess Persuasion, while another goddess and human wedding attendants make preparations.

Under Roman law, there were two different sorts of marriage. In the first, which was known as marriage **cum manū**, the bride ceased to be a member of her father's family and passed completely into the **manus** (hand, i.e. control) of her husband; any property she possessed became her husband's, and although he could divorce her, she could not divorce him. A couple could enter into marriage cum manu in various ways; one was by an ancient ceremony known as **cōnfarreātiō**, in which the bride and bridegroom together ate a sacred cake made of **far** (grain). This ceremony was used only by a few aristocratic families and had almost died out by the end of the first century AD; however, on p. 56, Polla is married by confarreatio because she is related to the Emperor Domitian.

By the first century, marriage cum manu had become far less common than the other type of marriage, which was known as marriage **sine manū**. In this type of marriage, the bride did not pass into the manus of her husband; legally, she was still regarded as a member of her father's family (even though she was now no longer living with them); she could possess property of her own and she could divorce her husband. It was very easy for a couple to enter into marriage sine manu; all they needed to do was to live together after declaring their intention of being man and wife.

Whether a couple became married cum manu or sine manu, they usually celebrated their wedding with some of the many customs and ceremonies that were traditional among the Romans. Some of these are mentioned in the story of Polla's wedding to Sparsus on pp. 56–9: the flame-coloured bridal veil (**flammeum**); the symbolic joining of hands (**iūnctiō dextrārum**); the sacrifice; the signing of the marriage contract, witnessed by the wedding guests; the wedding feast at the bride's house; the ancient custom of pretending to pull the bride away from her mother by force; the torch-lit procession to the bridegroom's house; the wedding song; the traditional words spoken by the bride to her husband, **ubi tū Gāius, ego Gāia** (*Where you are Gaius, I am Gaia*); and the custom of carrying the bride across the threshold of her new home. The watching crowd would shout their congratulations and make rude jokes to the bridegroom. Other traditions and ceremonies included the careful arrangement of the bride's hair, parted with the point of a spear and then divided into six plaits; the presentation of fire and water by the bridegroom to the bride; and the undressing of the bride by a **mātrōna ūnivira** (a woman who had had only one husband).

The chief purpose of Roman marriage, as stated in marriage contracts and in various laws, was the obvious one of producing and bringing up children. The Roman government often made efforts to encourage marriage and large families; in particular,

*Pictures of weddings very often show the joining of hands (*iūnctiō dextrārum*).*

A woman suckling her baby while her husband looks on.

the Emperor Augustus introduced a law which laid down penalties for those who remained unmarried (for example, by forbidding them to receive legacies) and offered special privileges to married couples who produced three or more children. Nevertheless, the birth rate in Rome dropped steadily from the second century BC onwards, especially among the senatorial class.

A Roman wife had fewer legal rights than her husband. In the eyes of the law, she was under the authority of either her husband or her father (or guardian), depending on whether she had been married *cum manu* or *sine manu*. She could not vote in elections, take an active part in public or political life, sit on a jury or plead in court. But in some ways a first-century Roman wife had more freedom than women in other countries, and enjoyed a higher status than they did. She was not restricted to the home, but could visit friends, go to the theatre and the baths, and accompany her husband to dinner-parties (unlike the women of classical Athens, for example). Her traditional day-to-day task – the running of the household – was regarded by most Romans as important and valuable, and a woman could gain great prestige and respect for the way in which this task was carried out; in many aristocratic and wealthy families, running the house was a highly complicated and demanding job, involving the management and supervision of a large number of domestic slaves.

Our knowledge of Roman married life is very incomplete. We know far less about the poor than about the wealthy upper classes, and have hardly any information on married life from

A wife could go to a party with her husband (painting in Pompeii).

the wife's point of view, because most of what is written in Latin was written by men. Nevertheless, the writings of Roman authors include many references to married life. The following letter, for example, was written by Pliny to his wife Calpurnia:

'The strength of my longing for you is hard to believe. Love is the reason above all others. Another reason is that we are not used to being separated. I spend most of the night awake, picturing you. During the day, at the times when I usually come to see you, my feet guide me to your room; then I turn sadly back, sick at heart.'

Calpurnia was Pliny's third wife. At the time of their marriage, she was about fifteen and he was in his early forties. In another letter, he writes about Calpurnia:

'From sheer affection for me, she keeps copies of my speeches, reads them over and over again and even learns them by heart. She is tortured with worry when I appear in court, and is overcome with relief when the case is over. Whenever I give a recitatio, she listens from behind a curtain waiting eagerly for comments of approval. As for my poems, she sets them to music and sings them, taught not by some musician but by love, the best of teachers.'

A letter by Cicero describes an incident from the stormy relationship between his brother Quintus and Quintus' wife Pomponia:

'We lunched at Arcanum. When we got there, Quintus said, perfectly politely, "Pomponia, you invite the women, and I'll get the slave-boys together". There was nothing to be cross about, as far as I could see, in either what he said or the way he said it. But, within everyone's hearing, Pomponia replied, "What, me? I'm only a stranger here!" – just because Quintus had made arrangements for the lunch without telling her, I suppose. "There you are," said Quintus. "That's what I have to put up with every day." I hid my feelings. We sat down to eat; she refused to join us. Quintus sent her some food from the table; she sent it back. The following day, Quintus told me that she had refused to sleep with him and had continued to behave as she had done at lunch-time.'

Roman married life is also referred to in numerous epitaphs, written in memory of husbands and wives. There are extracts from three of them below.

HERE LIES
AMYMONE,
WIFE OF MARCUS,
MOST GOOD AND
MOST BEAUTIFUL,
WOOL-SPINNER,
DUTIFUL, MODEST,
CAREFUL, CHASTE,
HOME-LOVING.

I HAVE
WRITTEN THESE
WORDS SO THAT
THOSE WHO READ
THEM MAY REALISE
HOW MUCH WE
LOVED EACH
OTHER.

TO MY DEAREST WIFE,
WITH WHOM I LIVED
TWO YEARS, SIX
MONTHS, THREE DAYS,
TEN HOURS.

Vocabulary checklist 38

certus, certa, certum	certain, infallible
prō certō habēre	know for certain
clam	secretly, in private
cōpiae, cōpiārum	forces
dextra, dextrae	right hand
ēripiō, ēripere, ēripuī, ēreptus	rescue, snatch away
familia, familiae	household
grātus, grāta, grātum	acceptable, pleasing
ignōrō, ignōrāre, ignōrāvī	not know of
iungō, iungere, iūnxī, iūnctus	join
lēx, lēgis	law
līmen, līminis	threshold, doorway
nūbō, nūbere, nūpsī	marry
orior, orīrī, ortus sum	rise, arise
polliceor, pollicērī,	
pollicitus sum	promise
prohibeō, prohibēre, prohibuī,	
prohibitus	prevent
queror, querī, questus sum	lament, complain about
regō, regere, rēxī, rēctus	rule
vereor, verērī, veritus sum	be afraid, fear
vērō	indeed
virgō, virginis	virgin

A beautiful marble container provided by one of the emperor's freedmen for the ashes of his wife, Vernasia Cyclas.

STUDIA

hērēdēs prīncipis

I

*in aulā Imperātōris, duo puerī in studiīs litterārum sunt occupātī. alter
puer, Titus nōmine, fābulam nārrāre cōnātur; alter, nōmine Pūblius,
intentē audit. adest quoque puerōrum rhētor, M. Fabius Quīntiliānus.
Titus Pūbliusque, fīliī Clēmentis ac frātrēs Pōllae, nūper hērēdēs
Imperātōris factī sunt.*   *5*

Titus: (*fābulam nārrāns*) deinde Iuppiter, rēx deōrum,
                     sceleribus hominum valdē offēnsus, genus
                     mortāle magnō dīluviō dēlēre cōnstituit.

*Titō nārrante, iānua subitō aperītur. ingreditur Epaphrodītus. puerī
anxiī inter sē aspiciunt; Quīntiliānus, cui Epaphrodītus odiō est,*   *10*
nihilōminus eum cōmiter salūtat.

Quīntiliānus: libenter tē vidēmus, Epaphro –
Epaphrodītus: (*interpellāns*) salvēte, puerī. salvē tū, M. Fabī.
                     hūc missus sum ut mandāta prīncipis nūntiem.
                     prīnceps vōbīs imperat ut ad sē quam celerrimē   *15*
                     contendātis.
Quīntiliānus: verba tua, mī Epaphrodīte, nōn intellegō. cūr
                     nōs ad Imperātōrem arcessimur?

*Epaphrodītus, nūllō respōnsō datō, puerōs Quīntiliānumque per aulam
ad Imperātōris tablīnum dūcit. puerī, timōre commōtī, extrā tablīnum*   *20*
haesitant.

studiīs: **studium** *study*
litterārum: **litterae** *literature*

genus mortāle *the human race*
dīluviō: dīluvium *flood*

Quīntiliānus:	(*timōrem suum dissimulāns*) cūr perturbāminī, puerī?
Pūblius:	bonā causā perturbāmur. Imperātor enim nōs sine dubiō castīgābit vel pūniet.
Quīntiliānus:	nimis timidus es, Pūblī. sī prūdenter vōs gesseritis, neque castīgābiminī neque pūniēminī.

25

castīgābit: castīgāre *scold, reprimand*
vōs gesseritis: sē gerere *behave, conduct oneself*

II

Quīntiliānus et puerī, tablīnum ingressī, Domitiānum ad mēnsam sedentem muscāsque stilō trānsfīgentem inveniunt. Domitiānus neque respicit neque quicquam dīcit. puerī pallēscunt.

muscās: musca *fly*
respicit: respicere *look up*

Domitiānus:	(*tandem respiciēns*) nōlīte timēre, puerī. vōs nōn pūnītūrus sum – nisi mihi displicueritis. (*muscam aliam trānsfīgit; dēnique, stilō dēpositō, puerōs subitō interrogat:*) quam diū discipulī M. Fabiī iam estis?
Titus:	(*haesitāns*) d-duōs mēnsēs, domine.
Domitiānus:	nōbīs ergō tempus est cognōscere quid didicerītis. (*ad Pūblium repente conversus*) Pūblī, quid herī docēbāminī?
Pūblius:	versūs quōsdam legēbāmus, domine, quōs Ovidius poēta dē illō dīluviō fābulōsō composuit.
Domitiānus:	itaque, versibus Ovidiānīs herī lēctīs, quid hodiē facitis?
Pūblius:	hodiē cōnāmur eandem fābulam verbīs nostrīs nārrāre.
Quīntiliānus:	ubi tū nōs arcessīvistī, domine, Titus dē īrā Iovis nārrātūrus erat.
Domitiānus:	fābula scīlicet aptissima! eam audīre velim. Tite, nārrātiōnem tuam renovā!
Titus:	(*fābulam timidē renovāns*) Iu-Iuppiter nimbōs ingentēs dē ca-caelō dēmittere cōnstituit. statim Aquilōnem in ca-cavernīs Aeoliīs inclūsit, et Notum līberāvit. quī madidīs ālīs ēvolāvit; ba-barba nimbīs gravābātur, undae dē capillīs fluēbant. simulatque Notus ēvolāvit, nimbī dēnsī ex aethere cum ingentī fragōre effūsī sunt. sed tanta erat Iovis īra ut imbribus caelī contentus nōn esset; auxilium ergō ā frātre Neptūnō petīvit. quī cum terram tridente percussisset, illa valdē tremuit viamque patefēcit ubi undae fluerent. statim flūmina ingentia per campōs apertōs ruēbant.
Domitiānus:	satis nārrāvistī, Tite. nunc tū, Pūblī, nārrātiōnem excipe.

5

displicueritis: displicēre *displease*

10

didicerītis: discere *learn*

fābulōsō: fābulōsus *legendary, famous*
Ovidiānīs: Ovidiānus *of Ovid*

15

20

nārrātiōnem: nārrātiō *narration*
nimbōs: nimbus *rain-cloud*
cavernīs: caverna *cave, cavern*
Aeoliīs: Aeolius *Aeolian*
inclūsit: inclūdere *shut up*
Notum: Notus *South wind*
ālīs: āla *wing*
gravābātur: gravāre *load, weigh down*
imbribus: imber *rain*
Neptūnō: Neptūnus *Neptune (god of the sea)*
tridente: tridēns *trident*
campōs: campus *plain*
excipe: excipere *take over*

25

30

35

Pūblius: iamque inter mare et tellūrem nūllum discrīmen
            erat; mare ubīque erat, neque ūlla lītora habēbat.
            hominēs exitium effugere cōnābantur. aliī montēs
            ascendērunt; aliī, in nāvibus sedentēs, per agrōs   40
            illōs rēmigāvērunt quōs nūper arābant; hic suprā
            segetēs aut tēcta vīllārum mersārum nāvigāvit;
            ille in summīs arboribus piscēs invēnit. lupī inter
            ovēs natābant; leōnēs fulvī undīs vehēbantur.
            avēs, postquam terram diū quaerēbant ubi   45
            cōnsistere possent, tandem in mare fessīs ālīs
            dēcidērunt. capellae gracilēs –

Pūbliō hoc nārrantī Domitiānus manū significat ut dēsistat. diū tacet,
puerīs anxiīs exspectantibus; tandem loquitur.

Domitiānus: fortūnātī estis, Pūblī ac Tite; nam, ut decōrum est   50
             prīncipis hērēdibus, ab optimō rhētore docēminī,
             quī optima exempla vōbīs prōposuit. sī vōs, puerī,
             causās vestrās tam fācundē dīxeritis quam
             Ovidius versūs composuit, saepe victōrēs ē
             basilicā discēdētis; ab omnibus laudābiminī.   55
Titus: (*timōre iam dēpositō*) nōnne ūna rēs tē fallit,
             domine? nōs sumus hērēdēs tuī; nōnne igitur nōs,
             cum causās nostrās dīxerimus, nōn saepe sed
             semper victōrēs discēdēmus et ab omnibus
             laudābimur?   60

Quīntiliānus ērubēscit. Domitiānus, audāciā Titī obstupefactus, nihil
dīcit. tandem, rīdēns vel rīsum simulāns, puerōs rhētoremque dīmittit;
deinde, stilō resūmptō, muscās iterum trānsfīgere incipit.

ab omnibus laudābiminī.

About the language 1: passive and deponent verbs (continued)

1 Study the following examples:

> 'hērēdēs prīncipis' nunc **appellāmur**.
> *We **are** now **called** 'heirs of the emperor'.*

> cavēte, cīvēs! ab hostibus **dēcipiminī**.
> *Be careful, citizens!* ***You are being fooled*** *by the enemy.*

The words in **bold type** are passive forms of the 1st and 2nd persons plural.

2 Compare the active and passive forms of the 1st person plural:

	active	passive
present	portāmus	portāmur
	we carry	*we are carried*
future	portābimus	portābimur
	we shall carry	*we shall be carried*
imperfect	portābāmus	portābāmur
	we were carrying	*we were being carried*

Further examples:

a cūr ad aulam arcessimur? ab Imperātōre interrogābimur?
b ab omnibus amīcīs dēserēbāmur; ab ūnō servō fidēlī adiuvāmur.
c superāmur, prohibēbimur, dūcēbāmur, monēbimur, iubēmur, trahēbāmur.

3 Compare the active and passive forms of the 2nd person plural:

	active	passive
present	portātis	portāminī
	you carry	*you are carried*
future	portābitis	portābiminī
	you will carry	*you will be carried*
imperfect	portābātis	portābāminī
	you were carrying	*you were being carried*

Further examples:

a heri dērīdēbāminī; hodiē honōrāminī.
b servābiminī, quod ab Epaphrodītō semper dēfendiminī.
c mittiminī, docēbiminī, audiēbāminī, docēminī, superābāminī, dēlectābiminī.

4 Compare the 1st and 2nd person plural forms of **portō** with those of the deponent verb **cōnor**:

	active	*passive*	*deponent*
present	portāmus	portāmur	cōnāmur
	we carry	*we are being carried*	*we try*
	portātis	portāminī	cōnāminī
	you carry	*you are being carried*	*you try*
future	portābimus	portābimur	cōnābimur
	we shall carry	*we shall be carried*	*we shall try*
	portābitis	portābiminī	cōnābiminī
	you will carry	*you will be carried*	*you will try*
imperfect	portābāmus	portābāmur	cōnābāmur
	we were carrying	*we were being carried*	*we were trying*
	portābātis	portābāminī	cōnābāminī
	you were carrying	*you were being carried*	*you were trying*

Further examples of 1st and 2nd person plural forms of deponent verbs:

a ubi vōs proficīscēbāminī, nōs regrediēbāmur.
b templum ipsum mox cōnspicābimur.
c loquimur, loquiminī, precābimur, suspicābiminī, sequēbāmur, hortābāminī.

Domitian needed to adopt Titus and Publius as his heirs because his own son by his wife Domitia had died. When these coins were issued, the infant was already dead. We can tell this because the child is called dīvus Caesar, the divine Caesar. Emperors and members of their families were often proclaimed as gods after death. The larger coin shows the little Caesar with his mother; the smaller one shows him among the stars.

versūs Ovidiānī

The story of the flood, told by Publius and Titus on pp. 68–70, is based on the following lines written by the poet Ovid. When you have read them, answer the questions on the next page. At the start of the extract, the god Jupiter is about to punish the human race for its wickedness by submerging the earth in a great flood.

prōtinus **Aeoliīs** Aquilōnem claudit in **antrīs***.
ēmittitque Notum; **madidīs** Notus ēvolat **ālīs**;
barba gravis nimbīs, **cānīs** fluit unda **capillīs**.
fit fragor; hinc **dēnsī** funduntur ab aethere **nimbī**.
nec **caelō** contenta **suō** est Iovis īra, sed illum   5
caeruleus frāter iuvat auxiliāribus undīs.
ipse tridente suō terram percussit, at illa
intremuit mōtūque viās patefēcit aquārum.
exspatiāta ruunt per apertōs **flūmina** campōs.
  iamque mare et tellūs nūllum discrīmen habēbant: 10
omnia pontus erant, dēerant quoque lītora pontō.
occupat hic collem, **cumbā** sedet alter **aduncā**
et dūcit rēmōs illīc, ubi nūper arābat;
ille suprā segetēs aut **mersae** culmina **vīllae**
nāvigat, hic **summā** piscem dēprendit in **ulmō**.   15
nat lupus inter ovēs, **fulvōs** vehit unda **leōnēs**,
quaesītīsque diū terrīs, ubi sistere possit,
in mare **lassātīs** volucris vaga dēcidit **ālīs**.
et, modo quā **gracilēs** grāmen carpsēre **capellae**,
nunc ibi **dēfōrmēs** pōnunt sua corpora **phōcae**.   20

antrīs: antrum *cave*
cānīs: cānus *white*
fit: fierī *be made, occur*
hinc *then, next*
caeruleus *from the deep blue sea*
iuvat: iuvāre *help, assist*
auxiliāribus: auxiliāris *additional*
intremuit: intremere *shake*
exspatiāta: exspatiārī *extend, spread out*
pontus *sea*
dēerant: dēesse *be lacking, be missing*
collem: collis *hill*
cumbā: cumba *boat*
aduncā: aduncus *curved*
illīc *there, in that place*
culmina: culmen *roof*
ulmō: ulmus *elm tree*
nat: nāre *swim*
lassātīs: lassāre *tire, weary*
vaga: vagus *wandering*
quā *where*
grāmen *grass*
carpsēre = carpsērunt: carpere *chew, nibble, crop*
dēfōrmēs: dēfōrmis *ugly, inelegant*
phōcae: phōca *seal*

* Some noun-and-adjective phrases, in which an adjective is separated by one word or more from the noun which it describes, are shown in **bold type**.

Questions

1 **prōtinus ... Notum** (lines 1–2). What two things did Jupiter do?   2
2 **madidīs ... capillīs** (lines 2–3). In this description of the South wind, how does Ovid emphasise that he brings rain? Make three points.   3
3 **fit ... nimbī** (line 4). What happened when the South wind appeared?   2
4 Who came to Jupiter's assistance (lines 5–6)? What was his name?   1
5 What did he do?   1
6 What results did this have (lines 7–9)?   4
7 How does Ovid emphasise the vastness of the flood (line 11)?   2
8 **dūcit rēmōs** (line 13). Where is this man rowing?   1
9 **ille ... nāvigat** (lines 14–15). Where is this one sailing?   1
10 **hic ... piscem dēprendit** (line 15). What is remarkable about this?   2
11 **nat lupus inter ovēs** (line 16). What is strange about the relationship of these animals?   2
12 **quaesītīs ... ālīs** (lines 17–18). What happened to the birds? Why?   1 + 2
13 What is the connection between the goats and seals (lines 19–20)?   2
14 Which Latin word in line 20 is used to contrast with **gracilēs** in line 19?   1
15 How does Ovid vary his subject matter? Give three examples taken from the text.   3

TOTAL   **30**

Questions for discussion

1 Which detail or incident in this passage can you picture most vividly?
2 Which seems to you to be the better description of Ovid's account: 'serious' or 'light-hearted'?

About the language 2: word order (continued)

1   In Stage 36, you met verse sentences like this:

> exigis ut **nostrōs** dōnem tibi, Tucca, **libellōs**.
> *You demand that I should give you my books, Tucca.*

The adjective **nostrōs** is separated from the noun which it describes (**libellōs**).

2   In Stage 39, you have met sentences in which one noun-and-adjective phrase is followed by another:

> *caeruleus frāter* iuvat **auxiliāribus undīs**.
> *His brother from the deep blue sea helps him with additional waves.*

Further examples:

a   *arbore* sub *magnā* **parva** latēbat **avis**.
b   *vertice* dē *summō* **liquidōs** mōns ēvomit **ignēs**.

  liquidōs: liquidus *liquid*
  ēvomit: ēvomere *spit out, spew out*

Study the pattern formed by the pairs of noun-and-adjective phrases in each of the above sentences. Similar patterns are often formed in English verse by rhymes at the ends of lines. For example:

> A man he was to all the country *dear*,
> And passing rich with forty pounds a *year*;
> Remote from towns he ran his godly **race**,
> Nor e'er had changed, nor wished to change his **place**.

3   You have also met sentences in which one noun-and-adjective phrase is placed inside another one:

> nunc ibi **dēfōrmēs** pōnunt *sua corpora* **phōcae**.
> *Now the ugly seals rest their bodies there.*

Further examples:

a   in **mediōs** vēnit *iuvenis fortissimus* **hostēs**.
b   cōnstitit ante **oculōs** *pulchra puella* **meōs**.

Compare the arrangement of the noun-and-adjective phrases in the previous sentences with the arrangement of the rhyming lines in such verse as the following:

> Ring out, wild bells, to the wild **sky**,
> The flying cloud, the frosty *light*;
> The year is dying in the *night*:
> Ring out, wild bells, and let him **die**.

4 In each of the following examples, pick out the Latin adjectives and say which nouns they are describing:

  a aure meā ventī murmura rauca sonant.
  The hoarse murmurs of the wind sound in my ear.
  b iam nova prōgeniēs caelō dēmittitur altō. (*Virgil*)
  Now a new generation is being sent down from high heaven.
  c nōn fuit ingeniō Fāma maligna meō. (*Ovid*)
  Fame has not been unkind to my talent.
  d agna lupōs audit circum stabula alta frementēs. (*Ovid*)
  The lamb hears the wolves howling around the tall sheepfolds.
  e atque opere in mediō laetus cantābat arātor.
  And the happy ploughman was singing in the middle of his work.
  f vincuntur mollī pectora dūra prece. (*Tibullus*)
  Hard hearts are won over by soft prayer.

5 Translate the following examples:

  a *A cry for help*
  at puer īnfēlīx mediīs clāmābat in undīs.
  b *An echo*
  reddēbant nōmen concava saxa meum.
  c *Travel plans*
  nunc mare per longum mea cōgitat īre puella. (*Propertius*)
  d *Evening*
  maiōrēsque cadunt altīs dē montibus umbrae. (*Virgil*)

concava: concavus *hollow*

Pick out the adjectives in each example and say which nouns they are describing.

Practising the language

1   In each sentence, replace the noun in **bold type** with the correct form of the noun in brackets. Then translate the sentence.

Use the table of nouns on pp. 104–5 to help you, if necessary; you may also need to consult the Vocabulary to find out the genitive singular of 3rd declension nouns, as a guide to forming the other cases.

a   subitō Pōlla **Flāviam** vīdit. (māter)
b   nūntius **uxōrī** epistulam trādidit. (fēmina)
c   senātōrēs ad aulam **Domitiānī** contendēbant. (Imperātor)
d   iuvenis **Agricolae** tōtam rem nārrāvit. (dux)
e   ingēns multitūdō **Rōmānōrum** in amphitheātrō conveniēbat. (cīvis)
f   poēta **audītōribus** paucōs versūs recitāvit. (amīcus)

2   Complete each sentence with the correct verb. Then translate the sentence.

a   fessus sum! cotīdiē ā centuriōne labōrāre . . . . (iubeor, teneor)
b   tū semper bene recitās; semper ā rhētore . . . . (parāris, laudāris)
c   nōlī dēspērāre, mī amīce! mox . . . . (spectāberis, līberāberis)
d   maximē gaudeō; crās enim ab Imperātōre . . . . (honōrābor, vituperābor)
e   cum in urbe habitārem, strepitū continuō . . . . (audiēbar, mittēbar, vexābar)
f   medicus tē sānāvit, ubi morbō gravī . . . . (afficiēbāris, dēcipiēbāris, dūcēbāris)

3 Translate the first sentence. Then change it from a direct statement to an indirect statement by completing the second sentence. Finally, translate the second sentence.

For example: hostēs advēnērunt.
     nūntius dīcit hostēs advēn... .
Translated and completed, this becomes:
    hostēs advēnērunt.
    The enemy have arrived.
    nūntius dīcit hostēs advēnisse.
    The messenger says that the enemy have arrived.

In sentences **a–c**, a perfect *active* infinitive is required. For examples of the way in which this infinitive is formed, see p. 36, paragraph 3.

a Imperātor sententiam mūtāvit.
  cīvēs crēdunt Imperātōrem sententiam mūtāv... .
b nautae nāvem ingentem comparāvērunt.
  mercātor dīcit nautās nāvem ingentem comparāv... .
c fabrī mūrum optimē refēcērunt.
  putō fabr... mūrum optimē refēc... .

In sentences **d–f**, a perfect *passive* infinitive is required. For examples of the way in which it is formed, see p. 41, paragraph 3. Note that the first part of this infinitive (e.g. **parātus** in **parātus esse**) changes its ending to agree with the noun it describes.

For example: epistulae missae sunt.
     crēdō epistulās miss... ....
Translated and completed, this becomes:
    epistulae missae sunt.
    The letters have been sent.
    crēdō epistulās missās esse.
    I believe that the letters have been sent.

d victima ā pontifice ēlēcta est.
  spectātōrēs putant victimam ā pontifice ēlēct... ....
e multī amīcī ad cēnam vocātī sunt.
  sciō multōs amīcōs ad cēnam vocāt... ....
f captīvus occīsus est.
  mīlitēs dīcunt captīv... occīs... ....

Authors, readers and listeners

After a Roman writer had recited his work to his patron or friends, or to a wider audience at a recitatio, as described in Stage 36, he had to decide whether or not to make it available to the general public. If he decided to go ahead, his next step was to have several copies made. If he or his patron owned some sufficiently educated slaves, they might be asked to make copies for the author to distribute among his friends; or the author might offer his work to the booksellers, whose slaves would make a number of copies for sale to the public.

Most Roman booksellers had their shops in the Argiletum, a street which ran between the Forum and the Subura. Books were fairly cheap; a small book of poems might cost 5 sesterces for an ordinary copy, 20 sesterces for a de-luxe edition made of high-quality materials. After the work had been copied, all money from sales of the book belonged to the booksellers, not to the author. We do not know whether the booksellers ever paid anything to an author for letting them copy his work.

One result of these arrangements for copying and selling books was that there was no such thing in Rome as a professional writer; no author could hope to make a living from his work. Some of the people who wrote books were wealthy amateurs like Pliny, who made most of his money as a landowner and wrote as a hobby; others, like Martial, depended on patrons for support.

Sometimes the emperor became an author's patron. For example, the poets Virgil and Horace were helped and encouraged first by the Emperor Augustus' friend Maecenas, and then by Augustus himself. Other authors, however, got into trouble with the emperor. Ovid, for instance, was sent into exile by Augustus because he had been involved in a mysterious scandal in the emperor's own family, and because he had written a poem entitled *Ars Amatoria* (*The Art of Love*), a witty and light-hearted guide for young men on the conduct of love affairs. This greatly displeased Augustus, who had introduced a number of laws for the encouragement of respectable marriage (see pp. 63–4), and Ovid was exiled to a distant part of the empire for the rest of his life. Under later emperors such as Domitian, it was safest for an author to publish nothing at all, or else to make flattering remarks about the emperor in his work, like Martial in the story on p. 20 (lines 6–9).

Some works of Latin literature reached a wide public. For example, thousands of people saw the comic plays of Plautus when they were performed in the theatre. But most Roman

The Argiletum, where the book shops were, is the long street emerging from the Forum at top left, passing through the narrow Forum Transitorium which Domitian began, and running down to the bottom right in the crowded Subura district.

Choosing a book.

authors wrote for a small, highly educated group of readers who were familiar not only with Latin literature, but also with the literature of the Greeks.

Schoolboys like Publius and Titus in the story on pp. 68–70 were introduced by their teachers to the study of both Greek and Roman authors. Quintilian, who wrote a book called *The Education of an Orator*, gives a long list of recommended authors, adding comments on each one. For example, he says that 'Ovid is light-hearted even on serious subjects, and too fond of his own cleverness, but parts of his work are excellent.'

In this way, Latin literature played an important part in Roman education. Roman education, in turn, played an important part in the writing of Latin literature. Most Roman authors had received a thorough training from a rhetor, who taught them how to express themselves persuasively, how to choose words that would have maximum effect on an audience, and how to organise a speech in accordance with fixed rules. This training had a great influence on the way Latin literature was written.

The most important difference between Latin and modern literature is that modern literature (except drama) is usually written for silent reading, whereas Latin literature was normally written to be read aloud. Two reasons for this have been mentioned already: first, the easiest way for an author to tell the public about his work was to read it aloud to them; second, most authors had received a long training in public speaking when

Above: *The poet Horace was given this farm in the Sabine Hills by his patron, Maecenas.*
Below: *A boy practising public speaking. Round his neck he wears a* bulla, *a child's locket containing an amulet.*

they were young, and this affected the way they wrote. There is a third reason: when a Roman read a book, he normally read it aloud, even if he was reading it to himself. Reading silently was unusual. Saint Augustine was amazed when he saw it done, and wrote a brief description of it:

> **cum legēbat, oculī dūcēbantur per pāginās et cor intellēctum rīmābātur, vōx autem et lingua quiēscēbant.**
> *When he was reading, his eyes glided over the pages, and his heart searched out the meaning, but his voice and tongue were at rest.*

The fact that Latin literature was written for speaking aloud, and not for silent reading, made a great difference to the way Roman authors wrote. They expressed themselves in ways that would sound effective when heard, not just look effective when read. For example, suppose a Roman author wished to say, in the course of a story:

The unfortunate boy did not see the dangers.

He might express this quite straightforwardly:

> **puer īnfēlīx perīcula nōn vīdit.**

But he might, especially in verse, prefer a more dramatic way of expressing himself. For instance, he might address the character in the story as if he were physically present, and put a question to him:

> **heu, puer īnfēlīx! nōnne perīcla* vidēs?**
> *Alas, unfortunate boy! Do you not see the dangers?*

On the printed page, especially in English translation, this style of writing may appear artificial and exaggerated to a modern reader, but when read aloud in Latin the effect can be very different. To read Latin literature silently is like looking at the score of a piece of music: the reader gets some idea of what the piece is like, but it needs to be performed aloud for full effect.

***perīcla** is a shortened form of **perīcula**, common in verse.

Domitian's palace

The Emperor Domitian was a great builder. He finished Vespasian's Colosseum and gave Rome a stadium and a new forum (the Forum Transitorium) as well as many smaller buildings. He restored much of Rome after a serious fire. But his greatest building was his own palace, on the Palatine Hill.

Fragment of a floor made by cutting white and coloured marbles and red and green porphyry to an elaborate pattern.

The side of the palace overlooking the Circus Maximus.

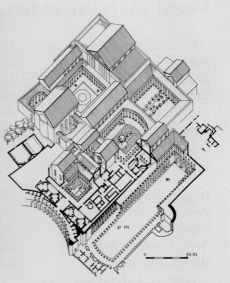

The palace reconstructed.

The Hippodrome: a garden in the shape of a stadium.

A wall belonging to the state rooms shown on p. 38, showing the holes for the builders' scaffolding. The builders constructed two brick walls and filled the gap between with mortar and rubble, i.e. concrete. The scaffolding holes would have been hidden by marble facing or stucco rendering.

Vocabulary checklist 39

arbor, arboris	*tree*
aut	*or*
cadō, cadere, cecidī	*fall*
campus, campī	*plain*
capillī, capillōrum	*hair*
discrīmen, discrīminis	*dividing line; crisis*
ergō	*therefore*
fallō, fallere, fefellī, falsus	*deceive, escape notice of, slip by*
fragor, fragōris	*crash*
genus, generis	*race*
hinc	*from here; then, next*
iuvō, iuvāre, iūvī	*help, assist*
littera, litterae	*letter (of alphabet)*
litterae, litterārum	*letter, letters (correspondence), literature*
mēnsis, mēnsis	*month*
simulō, simulāre, simulāvī, simulātus	*pretend*
stilus, stilī	*pen (pointed stick for writing on wax tablet)*
studium, studiī	*enthusiasm; study*
ūllus, ūlla, ūllum	*any*

*Domitian's palace:
connecting rooms leading
to the Hippodrome.*

IUDICIUM

STAGE 40

ingēns senātōrum multitūdō in cūriā convēnerat, ubi Gāius
Salvius Līberālis accūsābātur.

1 'multa scelera ā Salviō in Britanniā
commissa sunt.'

prīmus accūsātor affirmāvit multa scelera ā
Salviō in Britanniā commissa esse.

2 'Salvius testāmentum rēgis fīnxit.'

secundus accūsātor dīxit Salvium
testāmentum rēgis fīnxisse.

3 'innocēns sum.'

Salvius respondit sē innocentem esse.

accūsātiō

I

septimō annō Domitiānī prīncipātūs, C. Salvius Līberālis, quī
priōre annō fuerat cōnsul, ab Acīliō Glabriōne falsī accūsātus est.
quā rē imprōvīsā perturbātus, amīcōs statim cōnsuluit utrum
accūsātiōnem sperneret an dēfēnsiōnem susciperet.

    Salviō rogantī quid esset agendum, aliī alia suādēbant. aliī   5
affirmāvērunt nūllum perīculum īnstāre quod Salvius vir
magnae auctōritātis esset. aliī exīstimābant Domitiānī īram
magis timendam esse quam minās accūsantium; Salvium
hortābantur ut ad Imperātōrem īret veniamque peteret. amīcīs
dīversa monentibus, Salvius exspectāre cōnstituit, dum   10
cognōsceret quid Domitiānus sentīret.

    intereā Glabriō et aliī accūsātōrēs causam parābant. eīs
magnō auxiliō erat L. Mārcius Memor, haruspex et Salviī cliēns,
quī, socius quondam scelerum Salviī, nunc ad eum prōdendum
adductus est, spē praemiī vel metū poenārum. quō testimōniō   15
ūsī, accūsātōrēs rem ad Imperātōrem rettulērunt.

    Domitiānus, ubi verba accūsātōrum audīvit, cautē sē gessit;
bene enim sciēbat sē ipsum sceleribus Salviī implicārī. intereā, ut
speciem amīcitiae praebēret, Salvium dōnīs honōrāvit, ad cēnam
invītāvit, cōmiter excēpit.   20

accūsātiō *accusation*
prīncipātūs: prīncipātus
   principate, reign
falsī: falsum *forgery*
imprōvīsā: imprōvīsus
   unexpected, unforeseen
sperneret: spernere *ignore*
dēfēnsiōnem: dēfēnsiō
   defence
aliī alia ... *some ... one thing,*
   some ... another
īnstāre *be pressing, threaten*
minās: minae *threats*
dīversa: dīversus *different*
accūsātōrēs: accūsātor *accuser,*
   prosecutor
socius *companion, partner*
ad eum prōdendum *to betray*
   him
testimōniō: testimōnium
   evidence
implicārī: implicāre *implicate,*
   involve
speciem: speciēs *appearance*

II

Domitia autem, iam ab exiliō revocāta atque in favōrem Domitiānī restitūta, intentē ultiōnem adversus Salvium meditābātur. patefēcerat enim Myropnous pūmiliō Salvium auctōrem fuisse exiliī Domitiae, Paridis mortis; Salvium domum Hateriī falsīs litterīs Domitiam Paridemque invītāvisse; Salviō 5 auctōre, Domitiam in īnsulam duōs annōs relēgātam esse, Paridem occīsum esse.

accūsātōrēs igitur, ā Domitiā incitātī, cognitiōnem senātūs poposcērunt et impetrāvērunt. invidia Salviī aucta est suspīciōne Cogidubnum venēnō necātum esse. praetereā 10 nōnnūllī dīxērunt reliquiās corporum in thermīs Aquārum Sūlis inventās esse, dēfīxiōnēs quoque nōmine Cogidubnī īnscrīptās. quibus audītīs, multī crēdēbant Salvium dīs īnferīs inimīcōs cōnsecrāvisse.

tum dēmum Salvius intellēxit quantō in perīculō esset. veste 15 ergō mūtātā, domōs circumiit amīcōrum, quī sibi auxiliō essent. omnibus autem recūsantibus, domum rediit, spē omnī dēiectus.

restitūta: restituere *restore*
adversus *against*
domum Hateriī *to Haterius' house*
cognitiōnem senātūs: cognitiō senātūs *trial by the senate*
impetrāvērunt: impetrāre *obtain*
invidia *unpopularity*
reliquiās: reliquiae *remains*
dēfīxiōnēs: dēfīxiō *curse*
dīs īnferīs: dī īnferī *gods of the Underworld*
cōnsecrāvisse: cōnsecrāre *consecrate*
veste … mūtātā: vestem mūtāre *change clothing, i.e. put on mourning clothes*
circumiit: circumīre *go round, go around*

cognitiō

diē dictā, magna senātōrum multitūdō ad causam audiendam in cūriā convēnit. Salvius, iam metū cōnfectus, ad cūriam lectīcā vectus est; fīliō comitante, manibus extentīs, Domitiānō lentē ac suppliciter appropinquāvit. quī Salvium vultū compositō excēpit; crīminibus recitātīs, pauca dē Salviō ipsō addidit: eum 5 Vespasiānī patris amīcum fuisse, adiūtōremque Agricolae ā sē missum esse ad Britanniam administrandam. dēnique L. Ursum Serviānum, senātōrem clārissimum, ēlēgit quī cognitiōnī praeesset.

dictā: dictus *appointed*
ad causam audiendam *to hear the case, for the purpose of the case being heard*
cōnfectus *exhausted*
suppliciter *like a suppliant, humbly*
crīminibus: crīmen *charge*
adiūtōrem: adiūtor *assistant*

prīmō diē cognitiōnis Glabriō crīmina levia et inānia
exposuit. dīxit Salvium domī statuam suam in locō altiōre quam
statuam prīncipis posuisse; imāginem dīvī Vespasiānī quae
aulam rēgis Cogidubnī ōrnāvisset ā Salviō vīlī pretiō vēnditam
esse; et multa similia. quibus audītīs, Salvius spērāre coepit sē ē
manibus accūsātōrum ēlāpsūrum esse.

postrīdiē tamen appāruit accūsātor novus, Quīntus Caecilius
Iūcundus. vōce ferōcī, vultū minantī, oculīs ardentibus, verbīs
īnfestissimīs Salvium vehementer oppugnāvit. affirmāvit
Salvium superbē ac crūdēliter sē in Britanniā gessisse; cōnātum
esse venēnō necāre Ti. Claudium Cogidubnum, rēgem populō
Rōmānō fidēlissimum et amīcissimum; rēge mortuō, Salvium
testāmentum fīnxisse; poenās maximās meruisse.

Quīntō haec crīmina expōnentī ācriter respondit Salvius: 'id
quod dīcis absurdum est. quō modō venēnum Cogidubnō darī
potuit, tot spectātōribus adstantibus? quis tam stultus est ut
crēdat mē mortem rēgis octōgintā annōrum efficere voluisse?
etiam rēgēs mortālēs sunt.' dē testāmentō nihil explicāvit.

subitō extrā cūriam īnfestae vōcēs sunt audītae clāmantium
sē ipsōs Salvium interfectūrōs esse sī poenam scelerum
effūgisset. aliī effigiem Salviī dēreptam multīs contumēliīs in
Tiberim iēcērunt; aliī domum eius circumventam secūribus
saxīsque pulsāre coepērunt. tantus erat strepitus ut ēmitteret
prīnceps per urbem mīlitēs praetōriānōs quī tumultum sēdārent.

intereā Salvius, lectīcā vectus, ā tribūnō domum dēductus est;
utrum tribūnus custōs esset an carnifex, nēmō sciēbat.

10

15

20

25

30

35

levia: levis *trivial*
exposuit: expōnere *set out,*
explain
imāginem: imāgō *image, bust*

crūdēliter *cruelly*

amīcissimum: amīcus *friendly*
fīnxisse: fingere *forge*
meruisse: merēre *deserve*
ācriter *keenly, fiercely*

dēreptam: dēripere *tear down*

sēdārent: sēdāre *quell, calm*
down

About the language 1: indirect statement (concluded)

1   From Stage 35 onwards, you have met sentences in which indirect statements are introduced by a verb in the present tense, such as **dīcit**, **spērant**, **audiō**, etc.:

direct statements	*indirect statements*
'custōs revenit.'	puer dīcit custōdem revenīre.
'The guard is returning.'	*The boy says that the guard is returning.*
'puella recitābit.'	spērant puellam recitātūram esse.
'The girl will recite.'	*They hope that the girl will recite.*
'vīllae dēlētae sunt.'	audiō vīllās dēlētās esse.
'The villas have been destroyed.'	*I hear that the villas have been destroyed.*

2   In Stage 40, you have met sentences in which indirect statements are introduced by a verb in the perfect or imperfect tense, such as **dīxit**, **spērābant**, **audīvī**, etc.:

direct statements	*indirect statements*
'custōs revenit.'	puer dīxit custōdem revenīre.
'The guard is returning.'	*The boy said that the guard was returning.*
'puella recitābit.'	spērābant puellam recitātūram esse.
'The girl will recite.'	*They hoped that the girl would recite.*
'vīllae dēlētae sunt.'	audīvī vīllās dēlētās esse.
'The villas have been destroyed.'	*I heard that the villas had been destroyed.*

Compare the indirect statements in paragraph 1 with the indirect statements in paragraph 2. How do they differ?

3   Further examples:

a   'Salvius multa scelera commīsit.'
b   accūsātōrēs affirmāvērunt Salvium multa scelera commīsisse.
c   'mīlitēs urbem facile capient.'
d   centuriō crēdēbat mīlitēs facile urbem captūrōs esse.
e   'Agricola iniūstē revocātus est.'
f   multī senātōrēs putābant Agricolam iniūstē revocātum esse.
g   'frāter tuus in Britanniā iam habitat.'
h   nūntius dīxit frātrem meum in Britanniā illō tempore habitāre.
i   'Domitiānus timōre coniūrātiōnis saepe perturbātur.'
j   cīvēs sciēbant Domitiānum timōre coniūrātiōnis saepe perturbārī.

dēspērātiō

I

When you have read this part of the story, answer the questions at the end.

intereā Rūfilla, Salviī uxor, dum spēs eius firma manēbat,
pollicēbātur sē sociam cuiuscumque fortūnae futūram esse. cum
autem sēcrētīs Domitiae precibus veniam ā prīncipe
impetrāvisset, Salvium dēserere cōnstituit; dēnique mediā nocte
ē marītī cubiculō ēgressa domum patris suī rediit.   5

    tum dēmum Salvius dēspērābat. fīlius Vitelliānus identidem
affirmāvit senātōrēs numquam eum damnātūrōs esse; Salvium
hortābātur ut animō firmō dēfēnsiōnem postrīdiē renovāret.
Salvius autem respondit nūllam iam spem manēre: īnfestōs esse
senātōrēs, prīncipem nūllō modō lēnīrī posse.   10

    postulāvit tabulās testāmentī. quās signātās lībertō trādidit.
tum frēgit ānulum suum, nē posteā ad aliōs accūsandōs ūsuī
esset. postrēmō litterās in hunc modum compositās ad prīncipem
mīsit:

    'opprimor, domine, inimīcōrum coniūrātiōne mendācibusque 15
testibus, nec mihi licet innocentiam meam probāre. deōs
immortālēs testor mē semper in fidē mānsisse. hoc ūnum ōrō ut
fīliō meō innocentī parcās. nec quicquam aliud precor.'

    dē Rūfillā nihil scrīpsit.

dum *so long as*
firma: firmus *firm*
sociam: socia *companion, partner*
cuiuscumque: quīcumque *any, any whatever*

ūsuī esset: ūsuī esse *be of use*
mendācibus: mendāx *lying, deceitful*
mihi licet *I am allowed*
innocentiam: innocentia *innocence*
in fidē mānsisse: in fidē manēre *remain loyal*

Questions

		Marks
1	What did Rufilla at first promise?	2
2	Explain why she broke her promise (lines 2–4). Who was Domitia?	2 + 1
3	What suggests that Rufilla did not tell Salvius about her decision (lines 4–5)?	1
4	What effect did Rufilla's behaviour have on Salvius?	1
5	How did his son try to reassure him? What did he encourage him to do (lines 7–8)?	2 + 2
6	**Salvius … manēre** (line 9). Why did Salvius think this?	3
7	What did Salvius do after sealing and handing over his will?	1
	Explain why he did this (lines 11–13).	2
8	In his letter to the Emperor, Salvius explains the reasons for his downfall (lines 15–16). What were they?	2 + 2
9	What request did Salvius make to the Emperor in his letter (lines 17–18)?	
	What did he say about his wife?	2
10	Does this story change your previous opinion of Salvius? Give a reason.	2
	TOTAL	**25**

II

cum advesperāsceret, Salvius aliīs servīs pecūniam, aliīs
lībertātem dedit. deinde mortem sibi cōnscīscere parāvit. venēnō
ūtī nōn potuit; nam corpus iam diū antidotīs mūniēbātur.
cōnstituit ergō vēnās pugiōne incīdere. quō factō, in balneum
inlātus mox exanimātus est.   5

   at prīnceps, simulac mortem ā Salviō cōgitārī per ministrōs
cognōvit, tribūnum mīlitēsque domum eius ēmīsit. mandāvit eīs
ut Salviī mortem prohibērent; ipse enim crūdēlis vidērī nōlēbat.
mīlitēs igitur, ā tribūnō iussī, Salvium ē balneō extrāxērunt,
dēligāvērunt bracchia vulnerāta, sanguinem suppressērunt.   10

mortem sibi cōnscīscere
commit suicide
antidotīs: antidotum *antidote,*
remedy
mūniēbātur: mūnīre *protect,*
immunise
vēnās: vēna *vein*
incīdere *cut open*
suppressērunt: supprimere
staunch, stop flow of

damnātiō

damnātiō *condemnation*

postrīdiē Ursus Serviānus, quī cognitiōnī praefuerat, sententiam
prōnūntiāvit: nōmen Salviī Fāstīs ērādendum esse; bonōrum
eius partem pūblicandam, partem fīliō trādendam; Salvium
ipsum quīnque annōs relēgandum.

   ille igitur, vulneribus sānātīs, Rōmā discessit. eōdem diē   5
mīrum fideī exemplum oculīs populī Rōmānī obiectum est.
Q. Haterius Latrōniānus, quī favōrem Salviī flōrentis semper
quaerēbat, eum rēbus adversīs oppressum nōn dēseruit, sed in
exilium comitātus est.

   paucīs post diēbus Domitiānus accūsātōribus honōrēs ac   10
praemia distribuit. Glabriōnī sacerdōtium dedit; plūrimī autem
exīstimābant Glabriōnem rē vērā Domitiānum hāc accūsātiōne
graviter offendisse. Quīntō Caeciliō prīnceps favōrem suum ad
honōrēs petendōs pollicitus est; simul autem eum monuit nē
nimis ēlātus vel superbus fieret. pūmiliōnī Myropnoō, quī Salviī   15
scelera Domitiae patefēcerat, lībertātem obtulit; quam tamen ille
recūsāvit. 'quid mihi cum lībertāte?' rogāvit; 'satis est mihi
amīcum mortuum vindicāvisse.' et tībiīs dēmum resūmptīs,
exsultāns cantāre coepit.

sententiam: sententia *sentence*
prōnūntiāvit: prōnūntiāre
announce
Fāstīs: Fāstī *the list of consuls*
bonōrum: bona *goods,*
property
pūblicandam: pūblicāre
confiscate
flōrentis: flōrēre *flourish*

About the language 2: more about gerundives

1   In Stage 32, you met sentences like these:

> mihi fābula nārranda est.   Haterius laudandus est.
> *I must tell a story.*   *Haterius should be praised.*

In these examples, the gerundives **nārranda** and **laudandus** are being used with **est** to indicate that something *ought* to be done ('the story *ought* to be told', 'Haterius *ought* to be praised').

2   In Stage 40, you have met the gerundive used with **ad**, meaning *for the purpose of…*:

> deinde Quīntus ad Salvium accūsandum surrēxit.
> *Then Quintus stood up for the purpose of Salvius being accused.*
> Or, in more natural English:
> *Then Quintus stood up to accuse Salvius.*

> mercātōrēs in portū ad nāvem reficiendam manēbant.
> *The merchants stayed in port for the purpose of their ship being repaired.*
> Or, in more natural English:
> *The merchants stayed in port to repair their ship.*

3   Further examples:

a   Calēdoniī nūntiōs ad pācem petendam mīsērunt.
b   sculptor ingentem marmoris massam ad statuās faciendās comparāvit.
c   poēta ad versūs recitandōs scaenam ascendit.
d   Memor ad scelera Salviī patefacienda adductus est.
e   servōs in agrōs ad frūmentum colligendum ēmīsī.

dē tribus capellīs

The following poem by Martial is about a court case over the theft of three she-goats. However, the lawyer for the prosecution, Postumus, treats it as though it were a very important case requiring all his powers of oratory.

nōn dē vī neque caede nec venēnō,
sed līs est mihi dē tribus capellīs.
vīcīnī queror hās abesse fūrtō.
hoc iūdex sibi postulat probārī;
tū Cannās Mithridāticumque bellum   5
et periūria Pūnicī furōris
et Sullās Mariōsque Mūciōsque
magnā vōce sonās manūque tōtā.
iam dīc, Postume, dē tribus capellīs.

caede: caedēs *murder*
līs *court case*
fūrtō: fūrtum *theft*
Cannās: Cannae *Cannae, the site of a famous battle*
Mithridāticum bellum *the war with Mithridates*
periūria Pūnicī furōris *the frenzied treachery of Carthage,* literally, *the false oaths of Carthaginian frenzy*
Sullās, Mariōs … Mūciōs *people like Sulla, Marius and Mucius (famous Roman leaders)*
sonās: sonāre *sound off*
manū tōtā *with every kind of gesture,* literally, *with the whole hand*

Questions for discussion

1 How does Martial emphasise that the court case is about a trivial theft?
2 What kind of speech does the lawyer make (lines 5–8)? Why?
3 Why do you think Martial repeats the phrase **dē tribus capellīs** at the end of the poem?

A goat balanced improbably on a branch – a wall decoration from a villa near Pompeii.

Practising the language

1 Translate each sentence into Latin by selecting correctly from the list of Latin words.

a *I was being looked after by a very experienced doctor.*

ā medicō	perītiōre	cūrābam
prope medicum	perītissimō	cūrābar

b *The commander hopes that the messengers will return soon.*

lēgātus	spērō	nūntiī	mox	revenīre
lēgātī	spērat	nūntiōs	nūper	reventūrōs esse

c *We hear that a new house is being built.*

audīmus	domus	nova	aedificāre
audīvimus	domum	novam	aedificārī

d *After the conspiracy had been revealed* (two words only), *very many senators were condemned.*

coniūrātiōnem	patefactā	plūrimī	senātōrī	damnātī sunt
coniūrātiōne	patefactam	maximī	senātōrēs	damnātus est

e *The soothsayer advises you not to leave the city.*

haruspex	tū	monet	ut	urbī	discēdās
haruspicem	tē	monēbat	nē	ex urbe	discessissēs

2 With the help of paragraph 1 on p. 113, turn each of the following pairs of sentences into one sentence by replacing the word in **bold type** with the correct form of the relative pronoun **quī, quae, quod**. Then move the relative pronoun to the *beginning* of the relative clause. Finally translate the sentence. You may need to check the gender of the noun in the Vocabulary.

For example: intrāvit medicus. senex **medicum** arcessīverat.
This becomes: intrāvit medicus, **quem** senex arcessīverat.
*In came the doctor, **whom** the old man had sent for.*

a templum nōtissimum vīsitāvimus. Domitiānus ipse **templum** exstrūxerat.
b prō domō cōnsulis stābat pauper. praecō **pauperī** sportulam trādēbat.
c ille vir est Quīntus. pater **Quīntī** mēcum negōtium agere solēbat.
d servī flammās exstīnxērunt. vīlla **flammīs** cōnsūmēbātur.
e praemium illīs puerīs dabitur. auxiliō **puerōrum** fūr herī comprehēnsus est.

3 Complete each sentence with the correct verb. Then translate the sentence. Finally write down whether the sentence expresses a purpose, a result or an indirect command.

a iuvenis puellae persuādēre nōn poterat ut sēcum . . . . (fugeret, sperneret)

b senātōrēs tacēre cōnstituērunt nē Imperātōrem . . . . (offenderent, incēderent)

c tam fortis erās ut vērum dīcere nōn . . . . (funderēs, timērēs)

d tālis erat ille homō ut nēmō eī . . . . (crēderet, spērāret)

e uxōrēs ducem ōrābant nē captīvōs . . . . (interficeret, dēcideret)

f tam diū in vīllā rūsticā manēbam ut ad urbem regredī . . . . (sentīrem, nōllem)

g Domitiānus vōbīs imperat ut ad aulam statim . . . . (vincātis, conveniātis)

h vīsne mēcum ad theātrum venīre ut pantomīmum nōtissimum . . . .? (spectēmus, moveāmus)

Domitian

In this picture, Domitian is shown as a young man at the start of the principate of his father, Vespasian. Domitian is in the centre, welcoming Vespasian (right) to Rome.

When Vespasian became emperor he was campaigning overseas, and Domitian looked after affairs in Rome until his father could get back to the capital and take control himself. His critics said this experience gave Domitian a lust for power. When eventually he became emperor himself, he was a tyrant. He ignored the senate much of the time, relying on his inner circle of amici. Conspiracies against him were ruthlessly suppressed. Eventually he was assassinated by plotters including his wife, Domitia.

Roman law courts

At the beginning of the first century AD, there were several different law courts in Rome supervised by the praetors. If a Roman was charged with a criminal offence, he might find himself in one of a group of jury courts known as **quaestiōnēs** (commissions of inquiry), each responsible for judging a particular crime, such as treason, murder, adultery, misconduct by governors of provinces, forgery and election bribery. If he was involved in a civil (i.e. non-criminal) case, such as a dispute over a legacy, or an attempt to gain compensation from his next-door neighbour for damage to property, the case would be tried by a judge (**iūdex**). The iudex might be an ordinary citizen, with little knowledge of the law, but he could call on a panel of advisers to help him and could also ask legal experts (**iūris cōnsultī**) for their opinion.

By the time of Domitian, some further ways of handling law cases had been added. For example, a senator charged with a crime could be tried in the senate by fellow-senators, like Salvius in the story on pp. 87–92; and the emperor himself took an increasingly large part in administering the law (see p. 45). But the courts described in the previous paragraph continued to operate alongside these new arrangements.

In modern times, someone who has committed an offence is liable to be charged by the police and prosecuted by a lawyer who acts on behalf of the state; the system is supervised by a government department. In Rome, however, there were no charges by the police, no state lawyers and no government department responsible for prosecutions. If a man committed a crime, he could be prosecuted only by a private individual, not by a public official. Any citizen could bring a prosecution, and if the accused man was found guilty, there was sometimes a reward for the prosecutor.

The law courts played an important part in the lives of many Romans, especially senators and their sons. Success as a speaker in court was one of the aims of the long training which they received from the rhetor. In the law courts, a Roman could make a name for himself with the general public, play his part as a patron by looking after any clients who had got involved with the law, and perhaps impress influential people who might further his career.

Fame and prestige usually mattered more than financial reward to the men who conducted cases in the courts. For a long time, they were forbidden to receive payment at all from their clients. Later, they were permitted to accept a fee for their services, but this fee was regarded as an unofficial 'present', or

This coin illustrates voting in the senate: in the centre, under a canopy, the presiding magistrate's chair; on the right, the tablets used by the jurors (A and C); and on the left the urn into which they were cast.

donation, which the client was not obliged to pay and the lawyer was not supposed to ask for.

Roman courts were probably at their liveliest in the first century BC, when rival politicians fought each other fiercely in the courts as part of their struggle for power. By the time of Domitian, some of the glamour had faded; now that Rome was ruled by an emperor, there was less political power to be fought for. Nevertheless, the contests in court still mattered to the speakers and their clients, and attracted enthusiastic audiences. Pliny gives a vivid description of a case that aroused particularly lively interest:

> 'There they were, one hundred and eighty jurors, a great crowd of lawyers for both plaintiff and defendant, dozens of supporters sitting on the benches, and an enormous circle of listeners, several rows deep, standing round the whole courtroom. The platform was packed solid with people, and in the upper galleries of the basilica men and women were leaning over in an effort to hear, which was difficult, and see, which was rather easier.'

The writings of Martial, Pliny and Quintilian are full of casual details which convey the liveliness and excitement of the courts: the gimmicky lawyer who always wears an eye-patch while pleading a case; the hired squad of spectators who applaud at the right moments in return for payment; the successful speaker who wins a standing ovation from the jury; the careful allocation of time for each side, measured by the water-clock; the lawyer with the booming voice, whose speech is greeted by applause not only in his own court but also from the court next door; the windbag who is supposed to be talking about the theft of three she-goats, but goes off into long, irrelevant ramblings about Rome's wars with Carthage three hundred years ago (see the poem on p. 94); and the anxious wife who sends messengers to court every hour to find out how her husband is getting on.

It is difficult to say how fair Roman justice was. Some of the tactics used in Roman law courts had very little to do with the rights and wrongs of the case. An accused man might dress in mourning clothes or hold his little children up to the jury to arouse their pity. A speaker whose client was in the wrong might ignore the facts altogether, and try to win his case by appealing to the jury's emotions or prejudices, or by using irrelevant arguments. Sometimes a man might be accused and found guilty for political reasons; there were a number of 'treason trials' under Domitian, in which innocent men were condemned. However, the writings of such men as Pliny and Quintilian show that at least some Roman judges made an honest effort to be fair and just. Fairness in a Roman law court was partly the result of the laws themselves. Thanks largely to

Statue of a Roman making a speech.

the work of the iuris consulti, Roman law continued to evolve
and at its best it was careful, practical and immensely detailed.
Roman civil law, in particular, had an enormous influence on
mediaeval Europe and it still forms the basis of many present-
day legal systems in Europe and South America.

Remains of the Basilica Julia in the Forum, an important law court.
The case described by Pliny took place here. This is the building seen in
the background on p. 44.

Vocabulary checklist 40

affirmō, affirmāre, affirmāvī — *declare*
amīcitia, amīcitiae — *friendship*
augeō, augēre, auxī, auctus — *increase*
cōnsul, cōnsulis — *consul (senior magistrate)*

crīmen, crīminis — *charge*
cūria, cūriae — *senate-house*
dēmum — *at last*
    tum dēmum — *then at last, only then*
exīstimō, exīstimāre, exīstimāvī, exīstimātus — *think, consider*
inānis, ināne — *empty, meaningless*
invidia, invidiae — *jealousy, envy, unpopularity*

levis, leve — *light, slight, trivial*
minor, minārī, minātus sum — *threaten*
mūtō, mūtāre, mūtāvī, mūtātus — *change*
obiciō, obicere, obiēcī, obiectus — *present, put in the way of, expose to*

probō, probāre, probāvī — *prove*
prōdō, prōdere, prōdidī, prōditus — *betray*
similis, simile — *similar*
socius, sociī — *companion, partner*
suādeō, suādēre, suāsī — *advise, suggest*
ūtor, ūtī, ūsus sum — *use*
videor, vidērī, vīsus sum — *seem*

One of the boards for various games scratched on the steps of the Basilica Julia.

Language Information

Fragment of an inscription in Domitian's palace. There were once bronze letters set into the marble.

Contents

Part One: About the language

Nouns

1

	first declension	second declension			third declension
GENDER	f.	m.	m.	n.	m.
SINGULAR					
nominative and vocative	puella	servus (*voc.* serve)	puer	templum	mercātor
accusative	puellam	servum	puerum	templum	mercātōrem
genitive (of)	puellae	servī	puerī	templī	mercātōris
dative (to, for)	puellae	servō	puerō	templō	mercātōrī
ablative (by, with)	puellā	servō	puerō	templō	mercātōre
PLURAL					
nominative and vocative	puellae	servī	puerī	templa	mercātōrēs
accusative	puellās	servōs	puerōs	templa	mercātōrēs
genitive (of)	puellārum	servōrum	puerōrum	templōrum	mercātōrum
dative (to, for)	puellīs	servīs	puerīs	templīs	mercātōribus
ablative (by, with)	puellīs	servīs	puerīs	templīs	mercātōribus

	fourth declension		fifth declension
GENDER	f.	n.	m.
SINGULAR			
nominative and vocative	manus	genū	diēs
accusative	manum	genū	diem
genitive (of)	manūs	genūs	diēī
dative (to, for)	manuī	genū	diēī
ablative (by, with)	manū	genū	diē
PLURAL			
nominative and vocative	manūs	genua	diēs
accusative	manūs	genua	diēs
genitive (of)	manuum	genuum	diērum
dative (to, for)	manibus	genibus	diēbus
ablative (by, with)	manibus	genibus	diēbus

m.	m.	m.	f.	n.	n.	n.	GENDER
							SINGULAR
leō	cīvis	rēx	urbs	nōmen	tempus	mare	*nominative and vocative*
leōnem	cīvem	rēgem	urbem	nōmen	tempus	mare	*accusative*
leōnis	cīvis	rēgis	urbis	nōminis	temporis	maris	*genitive (of)*
leōnī	cīvī	rēgī	urbī	nōminī	temporī	marī	*dative (to, for)*
leōne	cīve	rēge	urbe	nōmine	tempore	marī	*ablative (by, with)*
							PLURAL
leōnēs	cīvēs	rēgēs	urbēs	nōmina	tempora	maria	*nominative and vocative*
leōnēs	cīvēs	rēgēs	urbēs	nōmina	tempora	maria	*accusative*
leōnum	cīvium	rēgum	urbium	nōminum	temporum	marium	*genitive (of)*
leōnibus	cīvibus	rēgibus	urbibus	nōminibus	temporibus	maribus	*dative (to, for)*
leōnibus	cīvibus	rēgibus	urbibus	nōminibus	temporibus	maribus	*ablative (by, with)*

2   For the ways in which the different cases are used, see pp. 126–7.

3   Compare the endings of **mare** with those of **nōmen** and **tempus**. Notice in particular the different form of the ablative singular. Other third declension neuter nouns whose nominative singular ends in **-e**, such as **conclāve** (*room*) and **cubīle** (*bed*), form their cases in the same way as **mare**.

4   Give the Latin for the nouns in *italic type* by forming the appropriate case of the word in **bold type**. If necessary, use the tables here and the Vocabulary on pp. 137–54 to help you with the declension and gender of the nouns.

    a   You have a very unusual *name*. (**nōmen**)
    b   The young man took the girl's *hands* in his. (**manus**)
    c   The informer told Epaphroditus an interesting *thing* about the senator. (**rēs**)
    d   The soldiers crossed several *rivers* on their march. (**flūmen**)
    e   The master discovered the *body of the young man* in the well. (**corpus, iuvenis**)
    f   Agricola quickly issued many *orders to the tribunes*. (**iussum, tribūnus**)
    g   Our men were spurred on *by the hope of victory*. (**spēs, victōria**)
    h   Domitian spent many *days* and *nights* thinking about his enemies. (**diēs, nox**)

Adjectives

1 *first and second declension*

SINGULAR	masculine	feminine	neuter	masculine	feminine	neuter
nominative and vocative	bonus (voc. bone)	bona	bonum	pulcher	pulchra	pulchrum
accusative	bonum	bonam	bonum	pulchrum	pulchram	pulchrum
genitive	bonī	bonae	bonī	pulchrī	pulchrae	pulchrī
dative	bonō	bonae	bonō	pulchrō	pulchrae	pulchrō
ablative	bonō	bonā	bonō	pulchrō	pulchrā	pulchrō
PLURAL						
nominative and vocative	bonī	bonae	bona	pulchrī	pulchrae	pulchra
accusative	bonōs	bonās	bona	pulchrōs	pulchrās	pulchra
genitive	bonōrum	bonārum	bonōrum	pulchrōrum	pulchrārum	pulchrōrum
dative	bonīs	bonīs	bonīs	pulchrīs	pulchrīs	pulchrīs
ablative	bonīs	bonīs	bonīs	pulchrīs	pulchrīs	pulchrīs

2 *third declension*

SINGULAR	masculine and feminine	neuter	masculine and feminine	neuter
nominative and vocative	fortis	forte	fēlīx	fēlīx
accusative	fortem	forte	fēlīcem	fēlīx
genitive	fortis	fortis	fēlīcis	fēlīcis
dative	fortī	fortī	fēlīcī	fēlīcī
ablative	fortī	fortī	fēlīcī	fēlīcī
PLURAL				
nominative and vocative	fortēs	fortia	fēlīcēs	fēlīcia
accusative	fortēs	fortia	fēlīcēs	fēlīcia
genitive	fortium	fortium	fēlīcium	fēlīcium
dative	fortibus	fortibus	fēlīcibus	fēlīcibus
ablative	fortibus	fortibus	fēlīcibus	fēlīcibus

third declension continued

SINGULAR	*masculine and feminine*	*neuter*	*masculine and feminine*	*neuter*
nominative and vocative	ingēns	ingēns	longior	longius
accusative	ingentem	ingēns	longiōrem	longius
genitive	ingentis	ingentis	longiōris	longiōris
dative	ingentī	ingentī	longiōrī	longiōrī
ablative	ingentī	ingentī	longiōre	longiōre
PLURAL				
nominative and vocative	ingentēs	ingentia	longiōrēs	longiōra
accusative	ingentēs	ingentia	longiōrēs	longiōra
genitive	ingentium	ingentium	longiōrum	longiōrum
dative	ingentibus	ingentibus	longiōribus	longiōribus
ablative	ingentibus	ingentibus	longiōribus	longiōribus

Comparatives and superlatives

Adjectives

1

	comparative	superlative
longus *long*	longior *longer*	longissimus *longest, very long*
pulcher *beautiful*	pulchrior *more beautiful*	pulcherrimus *most beautiful, very beautiful*
fortis *brave*	fortior *braver*	fortissimus *bravest, very brave*
fēlīx *lucky*	fēlīcior *luckier*	fēlīcissimus *luckiest, very lucky*
prūdēns *shrewd*	prūdentior *shrewder*	prūdentissimus *shrewdest, very shrewd*
facilis *easy*	facilior *easier*	facillimus *easiest, very easy*

2   Irregular forms

bonus *good*	melior *better*	optimus *best, very good*
malus *bad*	peior *worse*	pessimus *worst, very bad*
magnus *big*	maior *bigger*	maximus *biggest, very big*
parvus *small*	minor *smaller*	minimus *smallest, very small*
multus *much*	plūs *more*	plūrimus *most, very much*
multī *many*	plūrēs *more*	plūrimī *most, very many*

3   The forms of the comparative adjective **longior** are shown on p. 107.

4   Superlative adjectives such as **longissimus** change their endings in the same way as **bonus** (shown on p. 106).

Adverbs

1 Study the way in which comparative and superlative adverbs are formed:

	comparative	*superlative*
lātē *widely*	lātius *more widely*	lātissimē *most widely, very widely*
pulchrē *beautifully*	pulchrius *more beautifully*	pulcherrimē *most beautifully, very beautifully*
fortiter *bravely*	fortius *more bravely*	fortissimē *most bravely, very bravely*
fēlīciter *luckily*	fēlīcius *more luckily*	fēlīcissimē *most luckily, very luckily*
prūdenter *shrewdly*	prūdentius *more shrewdly*	prūdentissimē *most shrewdly, very shrewdly*
facile *easily*	facilius *more easily*	facillimē *most easily, very easily*

2 Irregular forms

bene *good*	melius *better*	optimē *best, very well*
male *badly*	peius *worse*	pessimē *worst, very badly*
magnopere *greatly*	magis *more*	maximē *most, very greatly*
paulum *little*	minus *less*	minimē *least, very little*
multum *much*	plūs *more*	plūrimum *most, very much*

3 Translate the following examples:

a mīlitēs nostrī fortius pugnāvērunt quam barbarī.
b faber mūrum facillimē refēcit.
c ubi strepitum audīvī, magis timēbam.
d optimē respondistī, mī fīlī.

Pronouns I: ego, tū, nōs, vōs, sē

1   ego and **tū** (*I, you,* etc.)

	SINGULAR		PLURAL	
nominative	ego	tū	nōs	vōs
accusative	mē	tē	nōs	vōs
genitive	meī	tuī	nostrum	vestrum
dative	mihi	tibi	nōbīs	vōbīs
ablative	mē	tē	nōbīs	vōbīs

2   sē (*himself, herself, themselves,* etc.)

	SINGULAR	PLURAL
accusative	sē	sē
genitive	suī	suī
dative	sibi	sibi
ablative	sē	sē

3   Note the adjectives that correspond to the pronouns in paragraphs 1 and 2:

meus, mea, meum	*my*	tuus, tua, tuum	*your* (s.)
noster, nostra, nostrum	*our*	vester, vestra, vestrum	*your* (pl.)
suus, sua, suum	*his own, her own,*		
	its own, their own		

These adjectives, like all other adjectives, agree with the nouns they describe in case, number and gender.

For example:

>   urbs vestra ā barbarīs mox dēlēbitur.
>   *Your city will soon be destroyed by the barbarians.*

>   domina līberōs suōs semper laudat.
>   *The mistress is always praising her own children.*

4   Give the Latin for the words in *italic type* in the following sentences:

a   The prisoner was led away *from us*.
b   *Our citizens* are very courageous.
c   He improved *his own villa*, but not his father's.
d   The welfare *of my slaves* is very important.
e   They wounded *themselves* to avoid being sent into battle.
f   I do not want to give anything *to you* (s.).
g   The patron gave money so that the villagers could have *their own temple*.
h   *You* (pl.) are rich, but *we* are happy.

Pronouns II: hic, ille, ipse, is, īdem

1 **hic** (*this*, *these*, etc.; also used with the meaning *he*, *she*, *they*, etc.)

	SINGULAR			PLURAL		
	masculine	*feminine*	*neuter*	*masculine*	*feminine*	*neuter*
nominative	hic	haec	hoc	hī	hae	haec
accusative	hunc	hanc	hoc	hōs	hās	haec
genitive	huius	huius	huius	hōrum	hārum	hōrum
dative	huic	huic	huic	hīs	hīs	hīs
ablative	hōc	hāc	hōc	hīs	hīs	hīs

2 **ille** (*that*, *those*, etc.; also used with the meaning *he*, *she*, *it*, etc.)

	SINGULAR			PLURAL		
	masculine	*feminine*	*neuter*	*masculine*	*feminine*	*neuter*
nominative	ille	illa	illud	illī	illae	illa
accusative	illum	illam	illud	illōs	illās	illa
genitive	illīus	illīus	illīus	illōrum	illārum	illōrum
dative	illī	illī	illī	illīs	illīs	illīs
ablative	illō	illā	illō	illīs	illīs	illīs

3 **ipse** (*myself*, *yourself*, *himself*, etc.)

	SINGULAR			PLURAL		
	masculine	*feminine*	*neuter*	*masculine*	*feminine*	*neuter*
nominative	ipse	ipsa	ipsum	ipsī	ipsae	ipsa
accusative	ipsum	ipsam	ipsum	ipsōs	ipsās	ipsa
genitive	ipsīus	ipsīus	ipsīus	ipsōrum	ipsārum	ipsōrum
dative	ipsī	ipsī	ipsī	ipsīs	ipsīs	ipsīs
ablative	ipsō	ipsā	ipsō	ipsīs	ipsīs	ipsīs

4 **is** (*he, she, it*, etc.; also used with the meaning *that, those*, etc.)

| | SINGULAR | | | PLURAL | | |
	masculine	*feminine*	*neuter*	*masculine*	*feminine*	*neuter*
nominative	is	ea	id	eī	eae	ea
accusative	eum	eam	id	eōs	eās	ea
genitive	eius	eius	eius	eōrum	eārum	eōrum
dative	eī	eī	eī	eīs	eīs	eīs
ablative	eō	eā	eō	eīs	eīs	eīs

Notice again how forms of **is** can also be used with the relative pronoun **quī**:

id quod mihi nārrāvistī statim Imperātōrī nūntiābitur.
What you have told to me will be reported at once to the Emperor.

eīs quī modo advēnērunt neque cibum neque pecūniam dabō.
To those who have just arrived I shall give neither food nor money.

5 **īdem** (*the same*)

| | SINGULAR | | | PLURAL | | |
	masculine	*feminine*	*neuter*	*masculine*	*feminine*	*neuter*
nominative	īdem	eadem	idem	eīdem	eaedem	eadem
accusative	eundem	eandem	idem	eōsdem	eāsdem	eadem
genitive	eiusdem	eiusdem	eiusdem	eōrundem	eārundem	eōrundem
dative	eīdem	eīdem	eīdem	eīsdem	eīsdem	eīsdem
ablative	eōdem	eādem	eōdem	eīsdem	eīsdem	eīsdem

Compare the forms of **īdem** with **is** in paragraph 4.

Pronouns III: **quī, quīdam**

1 The relative pronoun **quī** (*who, which,* etc.)

	SINGULAR			PLURAL		
	masculine	*feminine*	*neuter*	*masculine*	*feminine*	*neuter*
nominative	quī	quae	quod	quī	quae	quae
accusative	quem	quam	quod	quōs	quās	quae
genitive	cuius	cuius	cuius	quōrum	quārum	quōrum
dative	cui	cui	cui	quibus	quibus	quibus
ablative	quō	quā	quō	quibus	quibus	quibus

Notice again the use of the *connecting relative* at the beginning of sentences with the meaning *he, she, it, this,* etc.:

> rēx signum dedit. **quod** simulac vīdērunt, haruspicēs ad āram prōgressī sunt.
> *The king gave a signal. As soon as they saw **it**, the soothsayers advanced towards the altar.*

> cōnsul 'captīvīs parcere cōnstituī', inquit. **quibus** verbīs audītīs, senātōrēs plausērunt.
> *'I have decided to spare the prisoners', said the consul. On hearing **these** words, the senators applauded.*

2 From Stage 17 onwards, you have met various forms of the word **quīdam**, meaning *one, a certain*:

	SINGULAR			PLURAL		
	masculine	*feminine*	*neuter*	*masculine*	*feminine*	*neuter*
nominative	quīdam	quaedam	quoddam	quīdam	quaedam	quaedam
accusative	quendam	quandam	quoddam	quōsdam	quāsdam	quaedam
genitive	cuiusdam	cuiusdam	cuiusdam	quōrundam	quārundam	quōrundam
dative	cuidam	cuidam	cuidam	quibusdam	quibusdam	quibusdam
ablative	quōdam	quādam	quōdam	quibusdam	quibusdam	quibusdam

> quōsdam hominēs nōvī, quī tē adiuvāre poterunt.
> *I know certain men, who will be able to help you.*

> subitō senātor quīdam, celeriter prōgressus, silentium poposcit.
> *Suddenly one senator stepped forward quickly and demanded silence.*

Compare the forms of **quīdam** with **quī** in paragraph 1.

With the help of the table above, find the Latin for the words in *italic type* in the following sentences:

a *Certain* ladies were helping with the wedding preparations.
b *One* young man was addressing the crowd.
c I was staying at the house of *a certain* friend.

Verbs

Indicative active

1

		first conjugation	second conjugation	third conjugation	fourth conjugation
PRESENT		*I carry, you carry, etc.*	*I teach, you teach, etc.*	*I drag, you drag, etc.*	*I hear, you hear, etc.*
		portō	doceō	trahō	audiō
		portās	docēs	trahis	audīs
		portat	docet	trahit	audit
		portāmus	docēmus	trahimus	audīmus
		portātis	docētis	trahitis	audītis
		portant	docent	trahunt	audiunt
FUTURE		*I shall carry*	*I shall teach*	*I shall drag*	*I shall hear*
		portābō	docēbō	traham	audiam
		portābis	docēbis	trahēs	audiēs
		portābit	docēbit	trahet	audiet
		portābimus	docēbimus	trahēmus	audiēmus
		portābitis	docēbitis	trahētis	audiētis
		portābunt	docēbunt	trahent	audient
IMPERFECT		*I was carrying*	*I was teaching*	*I was dragging*	*I was hearing*
		portābam	docēbam	trahēbam	audiēbam
		portābās	docēbās	trahēbās	audiēbās
		portābat	docēbat	trahēbat	audiēbat
		portābāmus	docēbāmus	trahēbāmus	audiēbāmus
		portābātis	docēbātis	trahēbātis	audiēbātis
		portābant	docēbant	trahēbant	audiēbant

2 Translate each word, then change it from the singular to the plural, so that it means *we shall …* or *they will …* instead of *I shall …* or *s/he will …* . Then translate again.

nāvigābō; mittet; persuādēbit; impediam; monēbō; dūcam.

3 For ways of checking whether a verb ending in **-ēs**, **-et**, etc. belongs to the *present* tense of a *second* conjugation verb like **doceō** or the *future* tense of a *third* conjugation verb like **trahō**, see paragraph 3 on p. 136.

4

	first conjugation	*second conjugation*	*third conjugation*	*fourth conjugation*
PERFECT	*I (have) carried*	*I (have) taught*	*I (have) dragged*	*I (have) heard*
	portāvī	docuī	trāxī	audīvī
	portāvistī	docuistī	trāxistī	audīvistī
	portāvit	docuit	trāxit	audīvit
	portāvimus	docuimus	trāximus	audīvimus
	portāvistis	docuistis	trāxistis	audīvistis
	portāvērunt	docuērunt	trāxērunt	audīvērunt
FUTURE PERFECT	*I shall have carried*	*I shall have taught*	*I shall have dragged*	*I shall have heard*
	portāverō	docuerō	trāxerō	audīverō
	portāveris	docueris	trāxeris	audīveris
	portāverit	docuerit	trāxerit	audīverit
	portāverimus	docuerimus	trāxerimus	audīverimus
	portāveritis	docueritis	trāxeritis	audīveritis
	portāverint	docuerint	trāxerint	audīverint
PLUPERFECT	*I had carried*	*I had taught*	*I had dragged*	*I had heard*
	portāveram	docueram	trāxeram	audīveram
	portāverās	docuerās	trāxerās	audīverās
	portāverat	docuerat	trāxerat	audīverat
	portāverāmus	docuerāmus	trāxerāmus	audīverāmus
	portāverātis	docuerātis	trāxerātis	audīverātis
	portāverant	docuerant	trāxerant	audīverant

The future perfect is often translated by the English present tense:

> sī mē ad portum dūxeris, pecūniam tibi dabō.
> *If you take me to the harbour, I shall give you money.*

Indicative passive

1   In Stage 29, you met the following forms of the *passive*:

	first conjugation	*second conjugation*	*third conjugation*	*fourth conjugation*
PRESENT	*I am (being) carried*	*I am (being) taught*	*I am (being) dragged*	*I am (being) heard*
	portor	doceor	trahor	audior
	portāris	docēris	traheris	audīris
	portātur	docētur	trahitur	audītur
	portāmur	docēmur	trahimur	audīmur
	portāminī	docēminī	trahiminī	audīminī
	portantur	docentur	trahuntur	audiuntur
FUTURE	*I shall be carried*	*I shall be taught*	*I shall be dragged*	*I shall be heard*
	portābor	docēbor	trahar	audiar
	portāberis	docēberis	trahēris	audiēris
	portābitur	docēbitur	trahētur	audiētur
	portābimur	docēbimur	trahēmur	audiēmur
	portābiminī	docēbiminī	trahēminī	audiēminī
	portābuntur	docēbuntur	trahentur	audientur
IMPERFECT	*I was being carried*	*I was being taught*	*I was being dragged*	*I was being heard*
	portābar	docēbar	trahēbar	audiēbar
	portābāris	docēbāris	trahēbāris	audiēbāris
	portābātur	docēbātur	trahēbātur	audiēbātur
	portābāmur	docēbāmur	trahēbāmur	audiēbāmur
	portābāminī	docēbāminī	trahēbāminī	audiēbāminī
	portābantur	docēbantur	trahēbantur	audiēbantur

2   In paragraph 1, find the Latin for:

he is being dragged; you (s.) will be carried; you (pl.) were being heard; we are taught; they will be dragged; we shall be heard.

3   Translate each verb, then change it from the singular to the plural, so that it means *you (pl.)* … or *they* … instead of *you (s.)* … or *s/he* … . Then translate again.

audiēbāris; docēris; trahētur; portābitur; mittēbāris; amātur.

4   Notice how the first and second conjugations form the future passive tense in a different way from the third and fourth conjugations. Compare this with the future active tense on p. 114.

5

	first conjugation	second conjugation	third conjugation	fourth conjugation
PERFECT	*I have been carried, I was carried*	*I have been taught, I was taught*	*I have been dragged, I was dragged*	*I have been heard, I was heard*
	portātus sum	doctus sum	tractus sum	audītus sum
	portātus es	doctus es	tractus es	audītus es
	portātus est	doctus est	tractus est	audītus est
	portātī sumus	doctī sumus	tractī sumus	audītī sumus
	portātī estis	doctī estis	tractī estis	audītī estis
	portātī sunt	doctī sunt	tractī sunt	audītī sunt
FUTURE PERFECT	*I shall have been carried*	*I shall have been taught*	*I shall have been dragged*	*I shall have been heard*
	portātus erō	doctus erō	tractus erō	audītus erō
	portātus eris	doctus eris	tractus eris	audītus eris
	portātus erit	doctus erit	tractus erit	audītus erit
	portātī erimus	doctī erimus	tractī erimus	audītī erimus
	portātī eritis	doctī eritis	tractī eritis	audītī eritis
	portātī erunt	doctī erunt	tractī erunt	audītī erunt
PLUPERFECT	*I had been carried*	*I had been taught*	*I had been dragged*	*I had been heard*
	portātus eram	doctus eram	tractus eram	audītus eram
	portātus erās	doctus erās	tractus erās	audītus erās
	portātus erat	doctus erat	tractus erat	audītus erat
	portātī erāmus	doctī erāmus	tractī erāmus	audītī erāmus
	portātī erātis	doctī erātis	tractī erātis	audītī erātis
	portātī erant	doctī erant	tractī erant	audītī erant

6 The future perfect passive, like the future perfect active, is often translated by an English present tense:

> sī exercitus noster crās victus erit, hostēs oppidum capere poterunt.
> *If our army is defeated tomorrow, the enemy will be able to capture the town.*

7 Translate each example, then change it from the pluperfect to the perfect tense, keeping the same person and number (i.e. 1st person singular, etc.). Then translate each example again.

For example:

> **portātī erāmus** *we had been carried* becomes **portātī sumus** *we have been carried, we were carried*.

> doctus eram; audītī erant; missī erātis; accūsātī erāmus; rogātus erās; ducta erat.

Subjunctive active

1

	first conjugation	second conjugation	third conjugation	fourth conjugation
PRESENT	portem	doceam	traham	audiam
	portēs	doceās	trahās	audiās
	portet	doceat	trahat	audiat
	portēmus	doceāmus	trahāmus	audiāmus
	portētis	doceātis	trahātis	audiātis
	portent	doceant	trahant	audiant
IMPERFECT	portārem	docērem	traherem	audīrem
	portārēs	docērēs	traherēs	audīrēs
	portāret	docēret	traheret	audīret
	portārēmus	docērēmus	traherēmus	audīrēmus
	portārētis	docērētis	traherētis	audīrētis
	portārent	docērent	traherent	audīrent
PERFECT	portāverim	docuerim	trāxerim	audīverim
	portāverīs	docuerīs	trāxerīs	audīverīs
	portāverit	docuerit	trāxerit	audīverit
	portāverīmus	docuerīmus	trāxerīmus	audīverīmus
	portāverītis	docuerītis	trāxerītis	audīverītis
	portāverint	docuerint	trāxerint	audīverint
PLUPERFECT	portāvissem	docuissem	trāxissem	audīvissem
	portāvissēs	docuissēs	trāxissēs	audīvissēs
	portāvisset	docuisset	trāxisset	audīvisset
	portāvissēmus	docuissēmus	trāxissēmus	audīvissēmus
	portāvissētis	docuissētis	trāxissētis	audīvissētis
	portāvissent	docuissent	trāxissent	audīvissent

2   For ways in which the subjunctive is used see pp. 130–1.

Other forms of the verb

1

	carry!	*teach!*	*drag!*	*hear!*
IMPERATIVE				
SINGULAR	portā	docē	trahe	audī
PLURAL	portāte	docēte	trahite	audīte

2

	carrying	*teaching*	*dragging*	*hearing*
PRESENT PARTICIPLE	portāns	docēns	trahēns	audiēns

Present participles change their endings in the same way as **ingēns** (shown on p. 107), except that their ablative singular sometimes ends in **-e**, e.g. **portante**, **docente**.

PERFECT PASSIVE PARTICIPLE	*having been carried* portātus	*having been taught* doctus	*having been dragged* tractus	*having been heard* audītus

For examples of perfect active participles, see **Deponent verbs**, p. 121.

FUTURE PARTICIPLE	*about to carry* portātūrus	*about to teach* doctūrus	*about to drag* tractūrus	*about to hear* audītūrus

Perfect passive and future participles change their endings in the same way as **bonus** (shown on p. 106).

For examples of ways in which participles are used, see pp. 128–9.

3

PRESENT ACTIVE INFINITIVE	*to carry* portāre	*to teach* docēre	*to drag* trahere	*to hear* audīre
PRESENT PASSIVE INFINITIVE	*to be carried* portārī	*to be taught* docērī	*to be dragged* trahī	*to be heard* audīrī
PERFECT ACTIVE INFINITIVE	*to have carried* portāvisse	*to have taught* docuisse	*to have dragged* trāxisse	*to have heard* audīvisse
PERFECT PASSIVE INFINITIVE	*to have been carried* portātus esse	*to have been taught* doctus esse	*to have been dragged* tractus esse	*to have been heard* audītus esse
FUTURE ACTIVE INFINITIVE	*to be about to carry* portātūrus esse	*to be about to teach* doctūrus esse	*to be about to drag* tractūrus esse	*to be about to hear* audītūrus esse

For examples of ways in which infinitives are used to express indirect statements, see pp. 132–3.

4

GERUNDIVE	portandus	docendus	trahendus	audiendus

Gerundives change their endings in the same way as **bonus** (p. 106).

For ways in which the gerundive is used, see p. 134.

Deponent verbs

1

	first conjugation	second conjugation	third conjugation	fourth conjugation
PRESENT	*I try, I am trying*	*I promise, I am promising*	*I speak, I am speaking*	*I rise, I am rising*
	cōnor	polliceor	loquor	orior
	cōnāris	pollicēris	loqueris	orīris
	cōnātur	pollicētur	loquitur	orītur
	cōnāmur	pollicēmur	loquimur	orīmur
	cōnāminī	pollicēminī	loquiminī	orīminī
	cōnantur	pollicentur	loquuntur	oriuntur
FUTURE	*I shall try*	*I shall promise*	*I shall speak*	*I shall rise*
	cōnābor	pollicēbor	loquar	oriar
	cōnāberis	pollicēberis	loquēris	oriēris
	cōnābitur	pollicēbitur	loquētur	oriētur
	cōnābimur	pollicēbimur	loquēmur	oriēmur
	cōnābiminī	pollicēbiminī	loquēminī	oriēminī
	cōnābuntur	pollicēbuntur	loquentur	orientur
IMPERFECT	*I was trying*	*I was promising*	*I was speaking*	*I was rising*
	cōnābar	pollicēbar	loquēbar	oriēbar
	cōnābāris	pollicēbāris	loquēbāris	oriēbāris
	cōnābātur	pollicēbātur	loquēbātur	oriēbātur
	cōnābāmur	pollicēbāmur	loquēbāmur	oriēbāmur
	cōnābāminī	pollicēbāminī	loquēbāminī	oriēbāminī
	cōnābantur	pollicēbantur	loquēbantur	oriēbantur
PRESENT PARTICIPLE	*trying* cōnāns	*promising* pollicēns	*speaking* loquēns	*rising* oriēns
PRESENT INFINITIVE	*to try* cōnārī	*to promise* pollicērī	*to speak* loquī	*to rise* orīrī

2 In paragraph 1 find the Latin for:

you (s.) speak; we were trying; s/he was promising; they will rise; you (pl.) were speaking; we shall promise.

3 Translate the following examples:

cōnāminī; pollicēberis; oriēbātur; loquentur; precābar; sequimur.

4 Notice the two different ways in which the future tense of deponent verbs is formed and compare them with the future passive forms on p. 116.

	first conjugation	second conjugation	third conjugation	fourth conjugation
PERFECT	*I (have) tried*	*I (have) promised*	*I (have) spoken*	*I have risen, I rose*
	cōnātus sum	pollicitus sum	locūtus sum	ortus sum
	cōnātus es	pollicitus es	locūtus es	ortus es
	cōnātus est	pollicitus est	locūtus est	ortus est
	cōnātī sumus	pollicitī sumus	locūtī sumus	ortī sumus
	cōnātī estis	pollicitī estis	locūtī estis	ortī estis
	cōnātī sunt	pollicitī sunt	locūtī sunt	ortī sunt
FUTURE PERFECT	*I shall have tried*	*I shall have promised*	*I shall have spoken*	*I shall have risen*
	cōnātus erō	pollicitus erō	locūtus erō	ortus erō
	cōnātus eris	pollicitus eris	locūtus eris	ortus eris
	cōnātus erit	pollicitus erit	locūtus erit	ortus erit
	cōnātī erimus	pollicitī erimus	locūtī erimus	ortī erimus
	cōnātī eritis	pollicitī eritis	locūtī eritis	ortī eritis
	cōnātī erunt	pollicitī erunt	locūtī erunt	ortī erunt
PLUPERFECT	*I had tried*	*I had promised*	*I had spoken*	*I had risen*
	cōnātus eram	pollicitus eram	locūtus eram	ortus eram
	cōnātus erās	pollicitus erās	locūtus erās	ortus erās
	cōnātus erat	pollicitus erat	locūtus erat	ortus erat
	cōnātī erāmus	pollicitī erāmus	locūtī erāmus	ortī erāmus
	cōnātī erātis	pollicitī erātis	locūtī erātis	ortī erātis
	cōnātī erant	pollicitī erant	locūtī erant	ortī erant
PERFECT ACTIVE PARTICIPLE	*having tried* cōnātus	*having promised* pollicitus	*having spoken* locūtus	*having risen* ortus

Perfect active participles change their endings in the same way as **bonus** (shown on p. 106).

	first conjugation	second conjugation	third conjugation	fourth conjugation
PERFECT INFINITIVE	*to have tried* cōnātus esse	*to have promised* pollicitus esse	*to have spoken* locūtus esse	*to have risen* ortus esse

6 In paragraph 5 find the Latin for:

they tried; you (s.) had spoken; we have risen; he will have spoken; you (pl.) had promised; he rose.

7 Translate each example, then change it from the pluperfect to the perfect tense, keeping the same person and number (i.e. 1st person singular, etc.). Then translate the examples again.

For example: **cōnātus erās** *you had tried* becomes **cōnātus es** *you have tried, you tried*.
locūtus erat; cōnātus eram; pollicitī erāmus; profectī erātis; adepta erat.

Irregular verbs

1 Indicative

PRESENT	*I am* sum es est sumus estis sunt	*I am able* possum potes potest possumus potestis possunt	*I go* eō īs it īmus ītis eunt	*I want* volō vīs vult volumus vultis volunt	*I bring* ferō fers fert ferimus fertis ferunt	*I take* capiō capis capit capimus capitis capiunt
FUTURE	*I shall be* erō eris erit erimus eritis erunt	*I shall be able* poterō poteris poterit poterimus poteritis poterunt	*I shall go* ībō ībis ībit ībimus ībitis ībunt	*I shall want* volam volēs volet volēmus volētis volent	*I shall bring* feram ferēs feret ferēmus ferētis ferent	*I shall take* capiam capiēs capiet capiēmus capiētis capient
IMPERFECT	*I was* eram erās erat erāmus erātis erant	*I was able* poteram poterās poterat poterāmus poterātis poterant	*I was going* ībam ībās ībat ībāmus ībātis ībant	*I was wanting* volēbam volēbās volēbat volēbāmus volēbātis volēbant	*I was bringing* ferēbam ferēbās ferēbat ferēbāmus ferēbātis ferēbant	*I was taking* capiēbam capiēbās capiēbat capiēbāmus capiēbātis capiēbant
PERFECT	*I have been, I was* fuī fuistī fuit fuimus fuistis fuērunt	*I have been able, I was able* potuī potuistī potuit potuimus potuistis potuērunt	*I have gone, I went* iī iistī iit iimus iistis iērunt	*I (have) wanted* voluī voluistī voluit voluimus voluistis voluērunt	*I (have) brought* tulī tulistī tulit tulimus tulistis tulērunt	*I have taken, I took* cēpī cēpistī cēpit cēpimus cēpistis cēpērunt
FUTURE PERFECT	*I shall have been* fuerō fueris fuerit fuerimus fueritis fuerint	*I shall have been able* potuerō potueris potuerit potuerimus potueritis potuerint	*I shall have gone* ierō ieris ierit ierimus ieritis ierint	*I shall have wanted* voluerō volueris voluerit voluerimus volueritis voluerint	*I shall have brought* tulerō tuleris tulerit tulerimus tuleritis tulerint	*I shall have taken* cēperō cēperis cēperit cēperimus cēperitis cēperint

PLUPERFECT	*I had been*	*I had been able*	*I had gone*	*I had wanted*	*I had brought*	*I had taken*
	fueram	potueram	ieram	volueram	tuleram	cēperam
	fuerās	potuerās	ierās	voluerās	tulerās	cēperās
	fuerat	potuerat	ierat	voluerat	tulerat	cēperat
	fuerāmus	potuerāmus	ierāmus	voluerāmus	tulerāmus	cēperāmus
	fuerātis	potuerātis	ierātis	voluerātis	tulerātis	cēperātis
	fuerant	potuerant	ierant	voluerant	tulerant	cēperant

2 Subjunctive

PRESENT						
	sim	possim	eam	velim	feram	capiam
	sīs	possīs	eās	velīs	ferās	capiās
	sit	possit	eat	velit	ferat	capiat
	sīmus	possīmus	eāmus	velīmus	ferāmus	capiāmus
	sītis	possītis	eātis	velītis	ferātis	capiātis
	sint	possint	eant	velint	ferant	capiant
IMPERFECT						
	essem	possem	īrem	vellem	ferrem	caperem
	essēs	possēs	īrēs	vellēs	ferrēs	caperēs
	esset	posset	īret	vellet	ferret	caperet
	essēmus	possēmus	īrēmus	vellēmus	ferrēmus	caperēmus
	essētis	possētis	īrētis	vellētis	ferrētis	caperētis
	essent	possent	īrent	vellent	ferrent	caperent
PERFECT						
	fuerim	potuerim	ierim	voluerim	tulerim	cēperim
	fuerīs	potuerīs	ierīs	voluerīs	tulerīs	cēperīs
	fuerit	potuerit	ierit	voluerit	tulerit	cēperit
	fuerīmus	potuerīmus	ierīmus	voluerīmus	tulerīmus	cēperīmus
	fuerītis	potuerītis	ierītis	voluerītis	tulerītis	cēperītis
	fuerint	potuerint	ierint	voluerint	tulerint	cēperint
PLUPERFECT						
	fuissem	potuissem	iissem	voluissem	tulissem	cēpissem
	fuissēs	potuissēs	iissēs	voluissēs	tulissēs	cēpissēs
	fuisset	potuisset	iisset	voluisset	tulisset	cēpisset
	fuissēmus	potuissēmus	iissēmus	voluissēmus	tulissēmus	cēpissēmus
	fuissētis	potuissētis	iissētis	voluissētis	tulissētis	cēpissētis
	fuissent	potuissent	iissent	voluissent	tulissent	cēpissent

3 Infinitives

PRESENT	*to be* esse	*to be able* posse	*to go* īre	*to want* velle	*to bring* ferre	*to take* capere
PERFECT	*to have been* fuisse	*to have been able* potuisse	*to have gone* iisse	*to have wanted* voluisse	*to have brought* tulisse	*to have taken* cēpisse
FUTURE	*to be about to be* futūrus esse		*to be about to go* itūrus esse		*to be about to bring* lātūrus esse	*to be about to take* captūrus esse

4 Study the following *passive* forms of **ferō** and **capiō**:

PRESENT	*I am brought* feror ferris fertur ferimur feriminī feruntur	*I am taken* capior caperis capitur capimur capiminī capiuntur
FUTURE	*I shall be brought* ferar ferēris etc.	*I shall be taken* capiar capiēris etc.
IMPERFECT	*I was being brought* ferēbar ferēbāris etc.	*I was being taken* capiēbar capiēbāris etc.
PERFECT	*I have been brought* lātus sum lātus es etc.	*I have been taken, I was taken* captus sum captus es etc.
FUTURE PERFECT	*I shall have been brought* lātus erō lātus eris etc.	*I shall have been taken* captus erō captus eris etc.

PLUPERFECT	*I had been brought* lātus eram lātus erās etc.	*I had been taken* captus eram captus erās etc.
PERFECT PASSIVE PARTICIPLE	*having been brought* lātus	*having been taken* captus
PRESENT PASSIVE INFINITIVE	*to be brought* ferrī	*to be taken* capī
PERFECT PASSIVE INFINITIVE	*to have been brought* lātus esse	*to have been taken* captus esse

5 In paragraph 4, find the Latin for:

they are brought; I was being taken; you (s.) had been brought; you (pl.) are being taken.

What would be the Latin for the following?

they will be taken; we were being brought; he has been taken; she had been brought.

Uses of the cases

1 *nominative*
    captīvus clāmābat.   *The prisoner was shouting.*

2 *vocative*
    valē, **domine!**   *Goodbye, master!*

3 *accusative*
  a **pontem** trānsiimus.   *We crossed the bridge.*
  b **trēs hōrās** labōrābam.   *I was working for three hours.*
  c per **agrōs**; ad **vīllam**; in **forum**   *through the fields; to the house; into the forum*

For examples of the accusative used in indirect statement, see pp. 132–3.

4 *genitive*
  a māter **puerōrum**   *the mother of the boys*
  b plūs **pecūniae**   *more money*
  c vir **maximae virtūtis**   *a man of very great courage*

5 *dative*
  a **mīlitibus** cibum dedimus.   *We gave food to the soldiers.*
  b **vestrō candidātō** nōn faveō.   *I do not support your candidate.*
  c Note this use of the dative of
      auxilium, **cūra** and **odium**:
        rēx nōbīs **magnō auxiliō** erat.   *The king was a great help to us.*
        dignitās tua mihi **cūrae** est.   *Your dignity is a matter of concern to me.*
        Epaphrodītus omnibus **odiō** est.   *Epaphroditus is hateful to everyone.*
                            Or, in more natural English:
                            Everyone hates Epaphroditus.

6 *ablative*
  a **spectāculō** attonitus   *astonished by the sight*
  b senex **longā barbā**   *an old man with a long beard*
  c **nōbilī gente** nātus   *born from a noble family*
  d **quārtō diē** revēnit.   *He came back on the fourth day.*
  e cum **amīcīs**; ab **urbe**; in **forō**   *with friends; away from the city; in the forum*
  f Note this use of the ablative:
      marītus erat ignāvior **uxōre**.   *The husband was lazier than his wife.*
      Compare this with another way
      of expressing the same idea:
      marītus erat ignāvior quam uxor.
  g The ablative is used with adjectives
      such as **dignus** (*worthy*) and **plēnus**
      (*full*), and verbs such as **ūtor** (*I use*):
      magnō honōre dignus   *worthy of great honour*
      venēnō ūtī cōnstituit.   *He decided to use poison.*

For examples of ablative absolute phrases, see paragraph 5 on p. 128.

7 Further examples of some of the uses listed above:

    a satis pecūniae habētis?
    b theātrum spectātōribus plēnum erat.
    c septem hōrās dormiēbam.
    d es stultior asinō!
    e mīlitēs gladiīs et pugiōnibus ūtēbantur.
    f Myropnous vōbīs auxiliō erit.
    g strepitū urbis cōnfectus, ad vīllam rūsticam discessit.
    h puella parentibus resistere nōn poterat.

Uses of the participle

1   From Book II onwards, you have seen how participles are used to describe nouns or pronouns:

> clientēs, sportulam adeptī, discessērunt.
> *The clients, having obtained their handout, departed.*

> centuriō tē in umbrā latentem vīdit.
> *The centurion saw you hiding in the shadow.*

In the first example, the perfect active participle **adeptī** describes **clientēs**; in the second example, the present participle **latentem** describes **tē**.

2   Sometimes the noun or pronoun described by a participle is omitted.

> valdē perturbātus, ex urbe fūgit.
> *Having been thoroughly alarmed, he fled from the city.*

> moritūrī tē salūtāmus.
> *We, (who are) about to die, salute you.*

In examples like these, the ending of the verb (**fūgit**, **salūtāmus**, etc.) makes it clear that the participle refers to 'he', 'we', etc.

3   Sometimes the participle refers not to a particular person or thing but more vaguely to 'somebody' or 'some people':

> tū faciem sub aquā, Sexte, natantis habēs.
> *You have the face, Sextus, of (someone) swimming under water.*

> ārea plēna strepitū labōrantium erat.
> *The courtyard was full of the noise of (people) working.*

4   Notice again how a noun and participle in the dative case may be placed at the beginning of the sentence:

> Salviō dē uxōre rogantī nūllum respōnsum dedī.
> *To Salvius asking about his wife I gave no reply.*
> Or, in more natural English:
> *When Salvius asked about his wife, I gave him no reply.*

5   In Book IV you met ablative absolute phrases:

> senex, pecūniā cēlātā, fīliōs arcessīvit.
> *After hiding his money, the old man sent for his sons.*

> Epaphrodītō loquente, nūntius accurrit.
> *While Epaphroditus was speaking, a messenger came dashing up.*

6   Further examples:

   a flammīs exstīnctīs, dominus ruīnam īnspexit.
   b ubīque vōcēs poētam laudantium audiēbantur.
   c ā iūdice damnātus, in exilium iit.
   d fēmina, multōs cāsūs passa, auxilium nostrum petēbat.
   e servō haesitantī lībertātem praemiumque obtulī.
   f lībertus puerōs ab Imperātōre arcessītōs per aulam dūxit.
   g multīs clientibus comitantibus, senātor ad Forum profectus est.
   h ab hostibus captī, dē vītā dēspērābāmus.

Uses of the subjunctive

1   with **cum** (meaning *when*)

cum montēs trānsīrēmus, equitēs appropinquantēs vīdimus.
When we were crossing the mountains, we saw horsemen approaching.

2   *indirect question*

haruspicēs cognōscere cōnābantur num ōmina bona essent.
The soothsayers were trying to find out whether the omens were good.

omnēs rogant quis tantum scelus commīserit.
Everyone is asking who has committed so great a crime.

3   *purpose clause*

Domitiānus ipse aderat ut fābulam spectāret.
Domitian himself was present to watch the play.

mīlitēs ēmittet quī turbam dēpellant.
He will send out soldiers to drive the crowd away.

4   *indirect command*

Agricola Britannōs hortātus est ut mōrēs Rōmānōs discerent.
Agricola encouraged the Britons to learn Roman ways.

ducem ōrābimus nē captīvōs interficiat.
We shall beg the leader not to kill the prisoners.

5   *result clause*

barbarī eōs adeō terrēbant ut domōs suās dēserere cōnstituerent.
The barbarians were terrifying them so much that they decided to abandon their homes.

tantās dīvitiās adeptus est ut vīllam splendidam iam possideat.
He has obtained such great riches that he now owns a splendid villa.

6   with **dum** (*until*) and **priusquam** (*before*)

exspectābant dum centuriō signum daret.
They were waiting until the centurion should give the signal.
Or, in more natural English:
They were waiting for the centurion to give the signal.

nōbīs fugiendum est, priusquam custōdēs nōs cōnspiciant.
We must run away before the guards catch sight of us.

7 The following examples include all six uses of the subjunctive listed above, and all four subjunctive tenses (present, imperfect, perfect and pluperfect, listed on p. 118):

a senex, cum verba medicī audīvisset, testāmentum fēcit.
b mīlitibus persuādēbō ut marītō tuō parcant.
c latrōnēs mercātōrem occīdērunt priusquam ad salūtem pervenīret.
d tam benignus est rēx ut omnēs eum ament.
e dominus ad iānuam festīnāvit ut hospitēs exciperet.
f scīre volō quis fenestram frēgerit.

8 From Stage 37 onwards, you have met the subjunctive used in sentences like these:

> avārus timēbat **nē fūr aurum invenīret**.
> *The miser was afraid that a thief would find his gold.*

> vereor **nē inimīcī nostrī tibi noceant**.
> *I am afraid that our enemies may harm you.*

The groups of words in **bold type** are known as *fear clauses*. Note the translation of **nē** in these clauses.

Further examples:

a dominus verēbātur nē servī effugerent.
b timeō nē Britannī urbem mox capiant.

Indirect statement

1   From Stage 35 onwards, you have met *indirect statements*, expressed by a noun or pronoun in the *accusative* case and a verb in one of the following *infinitive* forms:

   a   *present active infinitive*
puto poētam optimē recitāre.
I think that the poet recites very well.
(Compare this with the direct statement: 'poēta optimē recitat.')

   b   *present passive infinitive*
servus crēdit multōs hospitēs invītārī.
The slave believes that many guests are being invited.
(Compare: 'multī hospitēs invītantur.')

   c   *perfect active infinitive*
cūr suspicāris Salvium testāmentum fīnxisse?
Why do you suspect that Salvius forged the will?
(Compare: 'Salvius testāmentum fīnxit.')

   d   *perfect passive infinitive*
scīmus multa oppida dēlēta esse.
We know that many towns have been destroyed.
(Compare: 'multa oppida dēlēta sunt.')

   e   *future active infinitive*
crēdō mīlitēs fidem servātūrōs esse.
I believe that the soldiers will keep their word.
(Compare: 'mīlitēs fidem servābunt.')

2   Further examples:

   a   audiō trēs senātōrēs damnātōs esse.
   b   ancilla dīcit dominum in hortō ambulāre.
   c   spērāmus ducem auxilium mox missūrum esse.
   d   nūntius affirmat Agricolam mīlitēs ad proelium īnstrūxisse.
   e   fēmina putat marītum in illō carcere tenērī.

3   Compare the following examples:

   a   Salvius dīcit sē in Ītaliā habitāre.
       (Direct statement: 'in Ītaliā habitō'.)
   b   Salvius dīcit eum in forō ambulāre.
       (Direct statement: 'in forō ambulat'.)

4   The indirect statements in paragraphs 1–3 are each introduced by a verb in the *present* tense (e.g. **puto**, **crēdit**). Note how the indirect statements in paragraph 1 are translated if they are introduced by a verb in the perfect or imperfect tense.

   a   putāvī poētam optimē recitāre.
       I thought the poet was reciting very well.
   b   servus crēdēbat multōs hospitēs invītārī.
       The slave believed that many guests were being invited.
   c   cūr suspicātus es Salvium testāmentum fīnxisse?
       Why did you suspect that Salvius had forged the will?
   d   scīvimus multa oppida dēlēta esse.
       We knew that many towns had been destroyed.
   e   crēdidī mīlitēs fidem servātūrōs esse.
       I believed that the soldiers would keep their word.

5   Further examples:

   a   Pōlla dīxit sē Helvidium semper amātūram esse.
   b   Glabriō putābat amīcum in vīllā rūsticā ōtiōsum esse.
   c   scīvistīne Agricolam ā Britanniā revocātum esse?
   d   audīvimus eum multōs versūs scurrīlēs scrīpsisse.
   e   Lupus affirmāvit sē ā multīs clientibus cotīdiē vexārī.

Gerundives

1 From Stage 24 onwards, you have met the gerundive used in sentences like these:

mihi manendum est.	*I must stay.*
Haterius culpandus est.	*Haterius ought to be blamed.*
dea nōbīs laudanda est.	*We ought to praise the goddess.*
exīstimō Agricolam dēmovendum esse.	*I think that Agricola ought to be dismissed.*

2 Further examples:

    a nōbīs in hāc vīllā dormiendum est.
    b mihi multae epistulae scrībendae sunt.
    c exīstimō captīvōs līberandōs esse.

3 In Stage 40 you met the gerundive used to express a purpose:

> mercātor ad negōtium agendum Rōmam contendit.
> *The merchant hurried to Rome for the purpose of business being done.*

  Or, in more natural English:

> *The merchant hurried to Rome to do business.*

> senātor saltātrīcēs ad hospitēs dēlectandōs condūxit.
> *The senator hired dancing-girls to delight his guests.*

Further examples:

    a sacerdōtēs ad victimam īnspiciendam ārae appropinquāvērunt.
    b multī cīvēs ad Mārtiālem audiendum convēnērunt.
    c lēgātus equitēs ad fugitīvōs necandōs ēmīsit.

Sentences with **dum** (meaning *while*)

1 From Stage 29 onwards, you have met **dum** used with the meaning *while*:

> dum cīvēs sacrificium spectant, iuvenis subitō prōsiluit.
> *While the citizens were watching the sacrifice, a young man suddenly leapt forward.*

> dum bellum in Britanniā geritur, rēs dīra Rōmae accidit.
> *While the war was being waged in Britain, a terrible disaster happened at Rome.*

Notice that in sentences like these **dum** is used with the *present* tense, even when the statement refers to the past.

Further examples: **a** dum custōdēs dormiunt, captīvī effūgērunt.
              b dum nūntius in līmine haesitat, Imperātor 'intrā!' clāmāvit.

2 For examples of **dum** used with the meaning *until*, see paragraph 6 on p. 130.

Numerals

I	ūnus	1	prīmus	first
II	duo	2	secundus	second
III	trēs	3	tertius	third
IV	quattuor	4	quārtus	fourth
V	quīnque	5	quīntus	fifth
VI	sex	6	sextus	sixth
VII	septem	7	septimus	seventh
VIII	octō	8	octāvus	eighth
IX	novem	9	nōnus	ninth
X	decem	10	decimus	tenth
XI	ūndecim	11		
XII	duodecim	12		
XIII	trēdecim	13		
XIV	quattuordecim	14		
XV	quīndecim	15		
XVI	sēdecim	16		
XVII	septendecim	17		
XVIII	duodēvīgintī	18		
XIX	ūndēvīgintī	19		
XX	vīgintī	20		
XXX	trīgintā	30		
XL	quadrāgintā	40		
L	quīnquāgintā	50		
LX	sexāgintā	60		
LXX	septuāgintā	70		
LXXX	octōgintā	80		
XC	nōnāgintā	90		
C	centum	100		
M	mīlle	1000		
MM	duo mīlia	2000		

Part Two: Vocabulary

Notes

1 Nouns, adjectives, verbs and prepositions are listed as in the Book IV Language Information section.

2 Verbs such as **crēdō**, **obstō**, etc., which are often used with a noun or pronoun in the dative case, are marked + *dat*.

Notice again how such verbs are used:

tibi crēdō.	*I put trust in you.*
	Or, *I trust you.*
turba nōbīs obstābat.	*The crowd was a hindrance to us.*
	Or, *The crowd hindered us.*

3 The *present* tense of *second* conjugation verbs like **doceō** has the same endings (except in the 1st person singular) as the *future* tense of *third* conjugation verbs like **trahō**.

For example:

	present		*future*	
active	doceam	*I teach*	traham	*I shall drag*
	docēs		**trahēs**	
	docet		**trahet**	
	etc.		etc.	
passive	doceor	*I am taught*	trahar	*I shall be dragged*
	docēris		**trahēris**	
	docētur		**trahētur**	
	etc.		etc.	

You can use the Vocabulary to check which conjugation a verb belongs to, and thus identify the tense correctly. For example, the conjugation and tense of **iubent** can be checked in the following way:

The verb is listed on p. 145 as **iubeō**, **iubēre**, etc., so it belongs to the second conjugation like **doceō**, **docēre**, etc. and therefore **iubent** must be in the present tense: *they order.*

And the conjugation and tense of **dūcent** can be checked like this:

The verb is listed on p. 141 as **dūcō**, **dūcere**, etc., so it belongs to the third conjugation like **trahō**, **trahere**, etc., and therefore **dūcent** must be in the future tense: *they will lead.*

Translate the following words, using pp. 137–54 to check conjugation and tense:

a rīdēs, intellegēs   c gaudēmus, monēmus   e prohibentur, regentur
b dēlent, venient   d convertet, ignōscet   f dūcēris, iubēris

4 All words which are given in the **Vocabulary checklists** for Stages 1–40 are marked with an asterisk(*).

a

A. = Aulus
* **ā, ab** + *abl.* — *from; by*
  abdūcō, abdūcere, abdūxī, abductus — *lead away*
* **abeō, abīre, abiī** — *go away*
  abripiō, abripere, abripuī, abreptus — *tear away from*
  abstineō, abstinēre, abstinuī — *abstain*
* **absum, abesse, āfuī** — *be out, be absent, be away*
  absurdus, absurda, absurdum — *absurd*
* **ac** — *and*
     idem ... ac — *the same ... as*
* **accidō, accidere, accidī** — *happen*
* **accipiō, accipere, accēpī, acceptus** — *accept, take in, receive*
  accurrō, accurrere, accurrī — *run up*
  accūsātiō, accūsātiōnis, f. — *accusation*
  accūsātor, accūsātōris, m. — *accuser, prosecutor*
* **accūsō, accūsāre, accūsāvī, accūsātus** — *accuse*
  acerbus, acerba, acerbum — *harsh, disagreeable*
  ācriter — *keenly, fiercely*
* **ad** + *acc.* — *to, at*
  addō, addere, addidī, additus — *add*
  addūcō, addūcere, addūxī, adductus — *lead, lead on, encourage*
* **adeō** — *so much, so greatly*
* **adeō, adīre, adiī** — *approach, go up to*
  adest *see* **adsum**
  adfīnis, adfīnis, m. — *relative, relation by marriage*
* **adhūc** — *up till now*
* **adipīscor, adipīscī, adeptus sum** — *receive, obtain*
  adiūtor, adiūtōris, m. — *helper, assistant*
* **adiuvō, adiuvāre, adiūvī** — *help, assist*
  administrō, administrāre, administrāvī, administrātus — *look after, manage*
  admīrātiō, admīrātiōnis, f. — *admiration*
  admoneō, admonēre, admonuī, admonitus — *warn, advise*
  adstō, adstāre, adstitī — *stand by*
* **adsum, adesse, adfuī** — *be here, be present*
  adsūmō, adsūmere, adsūmpsī, adsūmptus — *adopt*
  adulātiō, adulātiōnis, f. — *flattery*
  adulor, adulārī, adulātus sum — *flatter*
  aduncus, adunca, aduncum — *curved*
* **adveniō, advenīre, advēnī** — *arrive*
  adventus, adventūs, m. — *arrival*
  adversus + *acc.* — *against*
* **adversus, adversa, adversum** — *hostile, unfavourable*
* **rēs adversae** — *misfortune*
  advesperāscit, advesperāscere, advesperāvit — *get dark, become dark*
* **aedificium, aedificiī, n.** — *building*

* **aedificō, aedificāre, aedificāvī, aedificātus** — *build*
* **aeger, aegra, aegrum** — *sick, ill*
* **aequus, aequa, aequum** — *fair, calm*
  aestās, aestātis, f. — *summer*
  aetās, aetātis, f. — *age*
     aetāte flōrēre — *be in the prime of life*
  aethēr, aetheris, m. — *sky, heaven*
  afferō, afferre, attulī, adlātus — *bring*
* **afficiō, afficere, affēcī, affectus** — *affect, treat*
* **affectus, affecta, affectum** — *affected, overcome*
* **affirmō, affirmāre, affirmāvī** — *declare*
  afflīgō, afflīgere, afflīxī, afflīctus — *afflict, hurt*
* **ager, agrī, m.** — *field*
* **agitō, agitāre, agitāvī, agitātus** — *chase, hunt*
* **agmen, agminis, n.** — *column (of men), procession*
* **agnōscō, agnōscere, agnōvī, agnitus** — *recognise*
* **agō, agere, ēgī, āctus** — *do, act*
     age! — *come on!*
* **grātiās agere** — *thank, give thanks*
     quid agis? — *how are you? how are you getting on?*
     triumphum agere — *celebrate a triumph*
* **agricola, agricolae, m.** — *farmer*
  āla, ālae, f. — *wing*
  alacriter — *eagerly*
  aliquandō — *sometimes*
  aliquī, aliqua, aliquod — *some*
* **aliquis, aliquid** — *someone, something*
* **alius, alia, aliud** — *other, another, else*
     aliī alia ... — *some ... one thing, some ... another*
* **aliī ... aliī** — *some ... others*
* **alter, altera, alterum** — *the other, another, the second*
     alter ... alter — *one ... the other*
* **altus, alta, altum** — *high, deep*
* **ambō, ambae, ambō** — *both*
* **ambulō, ambulāre, ambulāvī** — *walk*
* **amīcitia, amīcitiae, f.** — *friendship*
* **amīcus, amīcī, m.** — *friend*
  amīcus, amīca, amīcum — *friendly*
* **āmittō, āmittere, āmīsī, āmissus** — *lose*
* **amō, amāre, amāvī, amātus** — *love, like*
* **amor, amōris, m.** — *love*
  amphitheātrum, amphitheātrī, n. — *amphitheatre*
  amplector, amplectī, amplexus sum — *embrace*
  amplius — *more fully, at greater length*
* **an** — *or*
* **utrum ... an** — *whether ... or*
* **ancilla, ancillae, f.** — *slave-girl, maid*
* **animadvertō, animadvertere, animadvertī, animadversus** — *notice, take notice of*

*animus, animī, m.	spirit, soul, mind
in animō volvere	wonder, turn over in the mind
*annus, annī, m.	year
*ante + *acc.*	before, in front of
*anteā	before
antidotum, antidotī, n.	antidote, remedy
antrum, antrī, n.	cave
*ānulus, ānulī, m.	ring
anxius, anxia, anxium	anxious
aper, aprī, m.	boar
*aperiō, aperīre, aperuī, apertus	open
*appāreō, appārēre, appāruī	appear
*appellō, appellāre, appellāvī, appellātus	call, call out to
*appropinquō, appropinquāre, appropinquāvī + *dat.*	approach, come near to
aptus, apta, aptum	suitable
*apud + *acc.*	among, at the house of
*aqua, aquae, f.	water
Aquilō, Aquilōnis, m.	North wind
*āra, ārae, f.	altar
*arbor, arboris, f.	tree
*arcessō, arcessere, arcessīvī, arcessītus	summon, send for
ardenter	passionately
*ardeō, ardēre, arsī	burn, be on fire
ārea, āreae, f.	courtyard, builder's yard
*arma, armōrum, n.pl.	arms, weapons
armātus, armāta, armātum	armed
arō, arāre, arāvī, arātus	plough
arripiō, arripere, arripuī, arreptus	seize
*ars, artis, f.	art, skill
*ascendō, ascendere, ascendī	climb, rise
ascīscō, ascīscere, ascīvī	adopt
asinus, asinī, m.	ass, donkey
aspiciō, aspicere, aspexī	look towards
assiduē	continually
*at	but
āthlēta, āthlētae, m.	athlete
*atque	and
ātrium, ātriī, n.	atrium, main room, hall
*attonitus, attonita, attonitum	astonished
attulī *see* afferō	
*auctor, auctōris, m.	creator, originator, person responsible
mē auctōre	at my suggestion
Salviō auctōre	at Salvius' suggestion
*auctōritās, auctōritātis, f.	authority
auctus *see* augeō	
*audācia, audāciae, f.	boldness, audacity
*audāx, *gen.* audācis	bold, daring
*audeō, audēre	dare
*audiō, audīre, audīvī, audītus	hear, listen to
audītor, audītōris, m.	listener; (pl.) audience
audītōrium, audītōriī, n.	auditorium, hall (used for public readings)

*auferō, auferre, abstulī, ablātus	take away, steal
*augeō, augēre, auxī, auctus	increase
*aula, aulae, f.	palace
auris, auris, f.	ear
aurum, aurī, n.	gold
*aut	or
*autem	but
auxiliāris, auxiliāre	additional
*auxilium, auxiliī, n.	help
auxiliō esse	be a help, be helpful
avārus, avārī, m.	miser
avis, avis, f.	bird
avus, avī, m.	grandfather

—————— **b** ——————

balneum, balneī, n.	bath
barba, barbae, f.	beard
barbarus, barbarī, m.	barbarian
barbarus, barbara, barbarum	barbarian
basilica, basilicae, f.	law court
*bellum, bellī, n.	war
* bellum gerere	wage war, campaign
Mithridāticum bellum	the war with Mithridates
bellus, bella, bellum	pretty
*bene	well
* optimē	very well
*benignus, benigna, benignum	kind
bēstia, bēstiae, f.	wild beast
*bibō, bibere, bibī	drink
bis	twice
*bonus, bona, bonum	good
bona, bonōrum, n.pl.	goods, property
* melior, melius	better
melius est	it would be better
* optimus, optima, optimum	very good, excellent, best
bracchium, bracchiī, n.	arm
*brevis, breve	short, brief
breviter	briefly
Britannī, Britannōrum, m.pl.	Britons
Britannia, Britanniae, f.	Britain

—————— **c** ——————

C. = Gāius	
cachinnō, cachinnāre, cachinnāvī	laugh, cackle
*cadō, cadere, cecidī	fall
caedes, caedis, f.	murder
*caelum, caelī, n.	sky, heaven

caeruleus, caerulea,
  caeruleum   *blue, from the deep blue sea*
Calēdonia, Calēdoniae, f.   *Scotland*
Calēdoniī, Calēdoniōrum,
  m.pl.   *Scots*
* callidus, callida, callidum   *clever, cunning, shrewd*
* campus, campī, m.   *plain*
* canis, canis, m.   *dog*
* cantō, cantāre, cantāvī   *sing, chant*
    tībiīs cantāre   *play on the pipes*
cantus, cantūs, m.   *song*
cānus, cāna, cānum   *white*
capella, capellae, f.   *she-goat*
* capillī, capillōrum, m.pl.   *hair*
* capiō, capere, cēpī, captus   *take, catch, capture*
* captīvus, captīvī, m.   *prisoner, captive*
* caput, capitis, n.   *head*
* carcer, carceris, m.   *prison*
* carmen, carminis, n.   *song*
carnifex, carnificis, m.   *executioner*
carpō, carpere, carpsī, carptus   *crop, chew, nibble*
* cārus, cāra, cārum   *dear*
casa, casae, f.   *small house*
castīgō, castīgāre, castīgāvī,
  castīgātus   *scold, reprimand*
* castra, castrōrum, n.pl.   *camp*
cāsus, cāsūs, m.   *misfortune*
catēna, catēnae, f.   *chain*
* causa, causae, f.   *reason, cause; case (of law)*
    causam dīcere   *plead a case*
cautē   *cautiously*
* caveō, cavēre, cāvī   *beware*
caverna, cavernae, f.   *cave, cavern*
* cēdō, cēdere, cessī   *give in, give way, make way*
celebrō, celebrāre, celebrāvī,
  celebrātus   *celebrate*
* celeriter   *quickly, fast*
    quam celerrimē   *as quickly as possible*
* cēlō, cēlāre, cēlāvī, cēlātus   *hide*
* cēna, cēnae, f.   *dinner*
* cēnō, cēnāre, cēnāvī   *dine, have dinner*
* centum   *a hundred*
centuriō, centuriōnis, m.   *centurion*
certē   *certainly*
certō, certāre, certāvī   *compete*
* certus, certa, certum   *certain, infallible*
*   prō certō habēre   *know for certain*
* cēterī, cēterae, cētera, pl.   *the others, the rest*
chorus, chorī, m.   *chorus, choir*
* cibus, cibī, m.   *food*
* circum + *acc.*   *around*
circumeō, circumīre, circumiī   *go round, go around*
* circumspectō,
  circumspectāre,
  circumspectāvī   *look round*
* circumveniō, circumvenīre,
  circumvēnī, circumventus   *surround*
* cīvis, cīvis, m.f.   *citizen*
* clam   *secretly, in private*
* clāmō, clāmāre, clāmāvī   *shout*

* clāmor, clāmōris, m.   *shout, uproar*
* clārus, clāra, clārum   *famous, distinguished, splendid*
* claudō, claudere, clausī,
  clausus   *shut, close, block,
                                                conclude, complete*
cliēns, clientis, m.   *client*
Cn. = Gnaeus
* coepī   *I began*
* cōgitō, cōgitāre, cōgitāvī   *think, consider*
cognāta, cognātae, f.   *relative (by birth)*
cognitiō, cognitiōnis, f.   *trial*
    cognitiō senātūs   *trial by the senate*
cognōmen, cognōminis, n.   *surname, additional name*
* cognōscō, cognōscere,
  cognōvī, cognitus   *get to know, find out*
* cōgō, cōgere, coēgī, coāctus   *force, compel*
colligō, colligere, collēgī,
  collēctus   *gather, collect, assemble*
collis, collis, m.   *hill*
collocō, collocāre, collocāvī,
  collocātus   *place, put*
colloquor, colloquī,
  collocūtus sum   *talk, chat*
colōnus, colōnī, m.   *tenant-farmer*
* comes, comitis, m.f.   *comrade, companion*
cōmiter   *politely, courteously*
* comitor, comitārī, comitātus
  sum   *accompany*
    comitāns, *gen.* comitantis   *accompanying*
commemorō, commemorāre,
  commemorāvī,
  commemorātus   *talk about, mention, recall*
commendō, commendāre,
  commendāvī,
  commendātus   *recommend*
committō, committere,
  commīsī, commissus   *commit, begin*
* commodus, commoda,
  commodum   *convenient*
* commōtus, commōta,
  commōtum   *moved, alarmed, excited,
                                                distressed, overcome*
* comparō, comparāre,
  comparāvī, comparātus   *obtain; compare*
* compleō, complēre,
  complēvī, complētus   *fill*
* complūrēs, complūra   *several*
* compōnō, compōnere,
  composuī, compositus   *put together, arrange, settle,
                                                compose*
    compositus, composita,
      compositum   *composed, steady*
* comprehendō,
  comprehendere,
  comprehendī,
  comprehēnsus   *arrest, seize*
cōnātur *see* cōnor
concavus, concava, concavum   *hollow*
condūcō, condūcere, condūxī,
  conductus   *hire*

cōnfarreātiō,
cōnfarreātiōnis, f.   *wedding ceremony*

*cōnficiō, cōnficere, cōnfēcī,
cōnfectus   *finish*

cōnfectus, cōnfecta,
cōnfectum   *worn out, exhausted,
overcome*

*cōnfīdō, cōnfīdere + *dat.*   *trust, put trust*

*coniciō, conicere, coniēcī,
coniectus   *hurl, throw*

coniūrātiō, coniūrātiōnis, f.   *plot, conspiracy*

*cōnor, cōnārī, cōnātus sum   *try*

cōnscīscō, cōnscīscere,
cōnscīvī   *inflict*

   mortem sibi cōnscīscere   *commit suicide*

cōnsecrō, cōnsecrāre,
cōnsecrāvī, cōnsecrātus   *consecrate*

*cōnsentiō, cōnsentīre,
cōnsēnsī   *agree*

cōnsīderātus, cōnsīderāta,
cōnsīderātum   *careful, well-considered*

cōnsīdō, cōnsīdere, cōnsēdī   *sit down*

*cōnsilium, cōnsiliī, n.   *plan, idea, advice, council*

*cōnsistō, cōnsistere, cōnstitī   *stand one's ground, stand firm,
halt, stop*

cōnsōlor, cōnsōlārī,
cōnsōlātus sum   *console*

*cōnspiciō, cōnspicere,
cōnspexī, conspectus   *catch sight of*

*cōnspicor, cōnspicārī,
cōnspicātus sum   *catch sight of*

*cōnstituō, cōnstituere,
cōnstituī, cōnstitūtus   *decide*

*cōnsul, cōnsulis, m.   *consul (senior magistrate)*

cōnsulāris, cōnsulāris, m.   *ex-consul*

*cōnsulō, cōnsulere, cōnsuluī,
cōnsultus   *consult*

*cōnsūmō, cōnsūmere,
cōnsūmpsī, cōnsūmptus   *eat*

*contendō, contendere,
contendī   *hurry*

*contentus, contenta,
contentum   *satisfied*

contineō, continēre, continuī   *contain*

contingō, contingere, contigī,
contāctus   *touch*

continuus, continua,
continuum   *continuous, on end*

*contrā + *acc.*   (1) *against*

*contrā   (2) *on the other hand*

contrahō, contrahere,
contrāxī, contractus   *draw together*

   supercilia contrahere   *draw eyebrows together,
frown*

contumēlia, contumēliae, f.   *insult, abuse*

*conveniō, convenīre, convēnī   *come together, gather, meet*

   in manum convenīre   *pass into the hands of*

*convertō, convertere,
convertī, conversus   *turn*

   sē convertere   *turn*

convertor, convertī,
conversus sum   *turn*

*cōpiae, cōpiārum, f.pl.   *forces*

*coquō, coquere, coxī, coctus   *cook*

*coquus, coquī, m.   *cook*

*corpus, corporis, n.   *body*

*cotīdiē   *every day*

*crās   *tomorrow*

*crēdō, crēdere, crēdidī + *dat.*   *trust, believe, have faith in*

*crīmen, crīminis, n.   *charge*

*crūdēlis, crūdēle   *cruel*

crūdēliter   *cruelly*

*cubiculum, cubiculī, n.   *bedroom*

cuiuscumque *see* quīcumque

culmen, culminis, n.   *roof*

*culpō, culpāre, culpāvī   *blame*

*cum   (1) *when*

   cum prīmum   *as soon as*

*cum + *abl.*   (2) *with*

cumba, cumbae, f.   *boat*

cūnctī, cūnctae, cūncta   *all*

Cupīdō, Cupīdinis, m.   *Cupid, god of love*

*cupiō, cupere, cupīvī   *want*

*cūr?   *why?*

*cūra, cūrae, f.   *care*

   cūrae esse   *be a matter of concern*

*cūria, cūriae, f.   *senate-house*

*cūrō, cūrāre, cūrāvī   *look after, supervise*

   nihil cūrō   *I don't care*

*currō, currere, cucurrī   *run*

*custōdiō, custōdīre,
custōdīvī, custōdītus   *guard*

*custōs, custōdis, m.   *guard*

——— **d** ———

damnātiō, damnātiōnis, f.   *condemnation*

damnō, damnāre, damnāvī,
damnātus   *condemn*

dare *see* dō

*dē + *abl.*   *from, down from; about, over*

*dea, deae, f.   *goddess*

*dēbeō, dēbēre, dēbuī,
dēbitus   *owe, ought, should, must*

*decem   *ten*

*dēcidō, dēcidere, dēcidī   *fall down*

decimus, decima, decimum   *tenth*

*dēcipiō, dēcipere, dēcēpī,
dēceptus   *deceive, fool, trick*

*decōrus, decōra, decōrum   *right, proper*

dedī *see* dō

dēdūcō, dēdūcere, dēdūxī,
dēductus   *escort*

dēeram *see* dēsum

*dēfendō, dēfendere, dēfendī,
dēfēnsus   *defend*

dēfēnsiō, dēfēnsiōnis, f.   *defence*

dēficiō, dēficere, dēfēcī — fail, die away

dēfīgō, dēfīgere, dēfīxī,
dēfīxus — fix

dēfīxiō, dēfīxiōnis, f. — curse

dēfōrmis, dēfōrme — ugly, inelegant

dēiciō, dēicere, dēiēcī,
dēiectus — throw down, throw

dēiectus, dēiecta,
dēiectum — disappointed, downcast

*deinde — then

*dēlectō, dēlectāre, dēlectāvī,
dēlectātus — delight, please

*dēleō, dēlēre, dēlēvī, dēlētus — destroy

dēliciae, dēliciārum, f.pl. — darling

dēligō, dēligāre, dēligāvī,
dēligātus — bind, tie, tie up, moor

*dēmittō, dēmittere, dēmīsī,
dēmissus — let down, lower

*dēmōnstrō, dēmōnstrāre,
dēmōnstrāvī, dēmōnstrātus — point out, show

dēmoveō, dēmovēre, dēmōvī,
dēmōtus — dismiss, move out of the way

*dēmum — at last

*   tum dēmum — then at last, only then

*dēnique — at last, finally

dēns, dentis, m. — tooth

dēnsus, dēnsa, dēnsum — thick

dēpellō, dēpellere, dēpulī,
dēpulsus — drive off, push down

dēpōnō, dēpōnere, dēposuī,
dēpositus — put down, take off

dēprehendō, dēprehendere,
dēprehendī, dēprehēnsus — discover

dēprendō = dēprehendō

dērīdeō, dērīdēre, dērīsī,
dērīsus — mock, jeer at

dēripiō, dēripere, dēripuī,
dēreptus — tear down

*dēscendō, dēscendere,
dēscendī — come down, go down

*dēserō, dēserere, dēseruī,
dēsertus — desert

dēsistō, dēsistere, dēstitī — stop

dēspērātiō, dēspērātiōnis, f. — despair

*dēspērō, dēspērāre,
dēspērāvī — despair, give up

dēsum, dēesse, dēfuī — be lacking, be missing

*deus, deī, m. — god

dī īnferī — gods of the Underworld

*dextra, dextrae, f. — right hand

*dīcō, dīcere, dīxī, dictus — say

causam dīcere — plead a case

dictus, dicta, dictum — appointed

dictō, dictāre, dictāvī, dictātus — dictate

didicī see discō

*diēs, diēī, m.f. — day

*difficilis, difficile — difficult

*dignitās, dignitātis, f. — dignity, importance,
prestige, honour

*dignus, digna, dignum — worthy, appropriate

*dīligenter — carefully, diligently

dīluvium, dīluviī, n. — flood

dīmittō, dīmittere, dīmīsī,
dīmissus — send away, dismiss

*dīrus, dīra, dīrum — dreadful

dīs see deus

*discēdō, discēdere, discessī — depart, leave

*discipulus, discipulī, m. — disciple, follower, pupil, student

*discō, discere, didicī — learn

*discrīmen, discrīminis, n. — crisis; boundary, dividing line

displiceō, displicēre,
displicuī + dat. — displease

dissentiō, dissentīre, dissēnsī — disagree, argue

dissimulō, dissimulāre,
dissimulāvī, dissimulātus — conceal, hide

distrahō, distrahere, distrāxī,
distractus — tear apart, tear in two

distribuō, distribuere,
distribuī, distribūtus — distribute

*diū — for a long time

dīversus, dīversa, dīversum — different

*dīves, gen. dīvitis — rich

*dīvitiae, dīvitiārum, f.pl. — riches

*dīvus, dīvī, m. — god

dīxī see dīcō

*dō, dare, dedī, datus — give

*   poenās dare — pay the penalty, be punished

*doceō, docēre, docuī, doctus — teach

*   doctus, docta, doctum — learned, educated,
skilful, clever

*doleō, dolēre, doluī — hurt, be in pain; grieve, be sad

*dolor, dolōris, m. — pain, grief

*domina, dominae, f. — mistress, madam

*dominus, dominī, m. — master

*domus, domūs, f. — house, home

domī — at home

domum Hateriī — to Haterius' house

*dōnō, dōnāre, dōnāvī,
dōnātus — give

*dōnum, dōnī, n. — present, gift

*dormiō, dormīre, dormīvī — sleep

*dubitō, dubitāre, dubitāvī — hesitate, doubt

nōn dubitō quīn — I do not doubt that

dubium, dubiī, n. — doubt

ducem see dux

ducentī, ducentae, ducenta — two hundred

*dūcō, dūcere, dūxī, ductus — lead, take

uxōrem dūcere — take as a wife, marry

*dum — while, until, so long as

*duo, duae, duo — two

duodecim — twelve

duodēvīgintī — eighteen

*dūrus, dūra, dūrum — harsh, hard

*dux, ducis, m. — leader

dūxī see dūcō

*ē, ex + *abl.* — *from, out of*
eandem *see* īdem
*ecce! — *see! look!*
efferō, efferre, extulī, ēlātus — *bring out, carry out*
  ēlātus, ēlāta, ēlātum — *excited, carried away*
*efficiō, efficere, effēcī, effectus — *carry out, accomplish*
effigiēs, effigiēī, f. — *image, statue*
*effugiō, effugere, effūgī — *escape*
*effundō, effundere, effūdī, effūsus — *pour out*
ēgī *see* agō
*ego, meī — *I, me*
  mēcum — *with me*
*ēgredior, ēgredī, ēgressus sum — *go out*
*ēheu! — *oh dear! oh no! alas!*
*ēiciō, ēicere, ēiēcī, ēiectus — *throw out*
eīdem *see* īdem
ēlābor, ēlābī, ēlāpsus sum — *slip out, escape*
ēlātus *see* efferō
ēlegāns, *gen.* ēlegantis — *tasteful, elegant*
*ēligō, ēligere, ēlēgī, ēlēctus — *choose*
*ēmittō, ēmittere, ēmīsī, ēmissus — *throw, send out*
*emō, emere, ēmī, ēmptus — *buy*
*enim — *for*
*eō, īre, iī — *go*
eōdem, eōsdem *see* īdem
epigramma, epigrammatis, n. — *epigram*
*epistula, epistulae, f. — *letter*
*eques, equitis, m. — *horseman, man of equestrian rank, (well-to-do man ranking below senator)*
equidem — *indeed*
equitō, equitāre, equitāvī — *ride*
*equus, equī, m. — *horse*
ērādō, ērādere, ērāsī, ērāsus — *rub out, erase*
eram *see* sum
*ergō — *therefore*
*ēripiō, ēripere, ēripuī, ēreptus — *snatch away, rescue*
errō, errāre, errāvī — *make a mistake; wander*
  longē errāre — *make a big mistake*
ērubēscō, ērubēscere, ērubuī — *blush*
ērumpō, ērumpere, ērūpī — *break away, break out*
esse, est *see* sum
*et — *and*
* et ... et — *both ... and*
*etiam — *even, also*
  nōn modo ... sed etiam — *not only ... but also*
ēvolō, ēvolāre, ēvolāvī — *fly out*
ēvolvō, ēvolvere, ēvolvī, ēvolūtus — *unroll, open*
ēvomō, ēvomere, ēvomuī, ēvomitus — *spit out, spew out*
*ex, ē + *abl.* — *from, out of*

exanimātus, exanimāta, exanimātum — *unconscious*
*excipiō, excipere, excēpī, exceptus — *receive, take over*
*excitō, excitāre, excitāvī, excitātus — *arouse, wake up, awaken*
*exclāmō, exclāmāre, exclāmāvī — *exclaim, shout*
excōgitō, excōgitāre, excōgitāvī, excōgitātus — *invent, think up*
excruciō, excruciāre, excruciāvī, excruciātus — *torture, torment*
exemplum, exemplī, n. — *example*
*exeō, exīre, exiī — *go out*
exerceō, exercēre, exercuī, exercitus — *exercise, practise, train*
*exercitus, exercitūs, m. — *army*
exigō, exigere, exēgī, exāctus — *demand*
exilium, exiliī, n. — *exile*
*exīstimō, exīstimāre, exīstimāvī, exīstimātus — *think, consider*
exitium, exitiī, n. — *ruin, destruction*
*explicō, explicāre, explicāvī, explicātus — *explain*
explōrātor, explōrātōris, m. — *scout, spy*
expōnō, expōnere, exposuī, expositus — *unload; set out, explain*
exspatior, exspatiārī, exspatiātus sum — *extend, spread out*
*exspectō, exspectāre, exspectāvī, exspectātus — *wait for*
extinguō, exstinguere, exstīnxī, exstīnctus — *extinguish, destroy, put out*
exstruō, exstruere, exstrūxī, exstrūctus — *build*
exsultō, exsultāre, exsultāvī — *exult, be triumphant*
extendō, extendere, extendī, extentus — *stretch out*
*extrā + *acc.* — *outside*
extrahō, extrahere, extrāxī, extractus — *drag out, pull out, take out*
*extrēmus, extrēma, extrēmum — *furthest*
  extrēma scaena — *the edge of the stage*

*faber, fabrī, m. — *craftsman, workman*
*fābula, fābulae, f. — *story, play*
fābulōsus, fābulōsa, fābulōsum — *legendary, famous*
facēs *see* fax
faciēs, faciēī, f. — *face*
*facile — *easily*
*facilis, facile — *easy*
*faciō, facere, fēcī, factus — *make, do*
  quid faciam? — *what am I to do?*
fācundē — *fluently, eloquently*

*fallō, fallere, fefellī, falsus	deceive, escape notice of, slip by
falsum, falsī, n.	lie, forgery
*falsus, falsa, falsum	false, untrue, dishonest
*familia, familiae, f.	household
familiāris, familiāris, m.	close friend, relation, relative
farreus, farrea, farreum	made from grain
Fāstī, Fāstōrum, m.pl.	the list of the consuls
*faveō, favēre, fāvī + dat.	favour, support
favor, favōris, m.	favour
fax, facis, f.	torch
febris, febris, f.	fever
fēcī see faciō	
fēlīciter!	good luck!
fēlīx, gen. fēlīcis	lucky
*fēmina, fēminae, f.	woman
fenestra, fenestrae, f.	window
*ferō, ferre, tulī, lātus	bring, carry
*ferōciter	fiercely
*ferōx, gen. ferōcis	fierce, ferocious
*fessus, fessa, fessum	tired
*festīnō, festīnāre, festīnāvī	hurry
*fidēlis, fidēle	faithful, loyal
*fidēs, fideī, f.	loyalty, trustworthiness
in fidē manēre	stay loyal
fīdus, fīda, fīdum	faithful
*fīlia, fīliae, f.	daughter
*fīlius, fīliī, m.	son
fingō, fingere, fīnxī, fictus	pretend, invent, forge
*fīnis, fīnis, m.	end
*fīō, fierī, factus sum	become, be made, occur
firmē	firmly
firmō, firmāre, firmāvī, firmātus	strengthen, establish
firmus, firma, firmum	firm
*flamma, flammae, f.	flame
flammeum, flammeī, n.	veil
flōreō, flōrēre, flōruī	flourish
aetāte flōrēre	be in the prime of life
*flōs, flōris, m.	flower
*flūmen, flūminis, n.	river
*fluō, fluere, flūxī	flow
foedus, foeda, foedum	foul, horrible
*fōns, fontis, m.	fountain, spring
forās	out of the house
*fortasse	perhaps
*forte	by chance
*fortis, forte	brave
*fortiter	bravely
fortūna, fortūnae, f.	fortune, luck
fortūnātus, fortūnāta, fortūnātum	lucky
forum, forī, n.	forum, market-place
*fragor, fragōris, m.	crash
*frangō, frangere, frēgī, frāctus	break
*frāter, frātris, m.	brother
*frūmentum, frūmentī, n.	grain
*frūstrā	in vain
*fuga, fugae, f.	escape
*fugiō, fugere, fūgī	run away, flee (from)
fugitīvus, fugitīvī, m.	fugitive, runaway
fuī see sum	
fulgeō, fulgēre, fulsī	shine, glitter
fulvus, fulva, fulvum	tawny
*fundō, fundere, fūdī, fūsus	pour
*fundus, fundī, m.	farm
*fūr, fūris, m.	thief
furor, furōris, m.	fury, frenzy
fūrtum, fūrtī, n.	theft
futūrus see sum	

g

*gaudeō, gaudēre	be pleased, rejoice
*gaudium, gaudiī, n.	joy
gelō, gelāre, gelāvī, gelātus	freeze
*gemitus, gemitūs, m.	groan
gemma, gemmae, f.	gem, jewel
gener, generī, m.	son-in-law
*gēns, gentis, f.	family, tribe, race
*genus, generis, n.	race
genus mortāle	the human race
Germānī, Germānōrum, m.pl.	Germans
Germānus, Germāna, Germānum	German
*gerō, gerere, gessī, gestus	wear; achieve
* bellum gerere	wage war, campaign
sē gerere	behave, conduct oneself
gladiātor, gladiātōris, m.	gladiator
*gladius, gladiī, m.	sword
glōria, glōriae, f.	glory
glōriōsus, glōriōsa, glōriōsum	boastful
gracilis, gracile	graceful
grāmen, grāminis, n.	grass
grātiae, grātiārum, f.pl.	thanks
* grātiās agere	give thanks, thank
*grātus, grāta, grātum	acceptable, pleasing
*gravis, grave	heavy, serious
*graviter	heavily, seriously, soundly
gravō, gravāre, gravāvī	load, weigh down

h

*habeō, habēre, habuī, habitus	have
* prō certō habēre	know for certain
*habitō, habitāre, habitāvī	live
haesitō, haesitāre, haesitāvī	hesitate
haruspex, haruspicis, m.	soothsayer
*hasta, hastae, f.	spear
*haud	not
*haudquāquam	not at all
hērēs, hērēdis, m.f.	heir
*heri	yesterday

Hibernī, Hibernōrum, m.pl.	*Irish*
Hibernia, Hiberniae, f.	*Ireland*
*hic, haec, hoc	*this*
hic ... ille	*this one ... that one, one man ... another man*
*hīc	*here*
*hinc	*from here; then, next*
Hispānia, Hispāniae, f.	*Spain*
*hodiē	*today*
*homō, hominis, m.	*human being, man*
homunculus, homunculī, m.	*little man*
*honor, honōris, m.	*honour, public position, official position*
honōrō, honōrāre, honōrāvī, honōrātus	*honour*
*hōra, hōrae, f.	*hour*
horrendus, horrenda, horrendum	*horrifying*
horrēscō, horrēscere, horruī	*shudder*
*hortor, hortārī, hortātus sum	*encourage, urge*
*hortus, hortī, m.	*garden*
*hospes, hospitis, m.	*guest, host*
*hostis, hostis, m.f.	*enemy*
*hūc	*here, to this place*
hūc ... illūc	*this way ... that way, one way ... another way*
humus, humī, f.	*ground*
* humī	*on the ground*
Hymēn, Hymenis, m.	*Hymen, god of weddings*
Hymenaeus, Hymenaeī, m.	*Hymen, god of weddings*

i

*iaceō, iacēre, iacuī	*lie*
*iaciō, iacere, iēcī, iactus	*throw*
*iactō, iactāre, iactāvī, iactātus	*throw*
*iam	*now*
*iānua, iānuae, f.	*door*
*ibi	*there*
*īdem, eadem, idem	*the same*
īdem ... ac	*the same ... as*
*identidem	*repeatedly*
ideō	*for this reason*
ideō ... quod	*for the reason that, because*
*igitur	*therefore, and so*
*ignārus, ignāra, ignārum	*not knowing, unaware*
*ignāvus, ignāva, ignāvum	*lazy, cowardly*
*ignis, ignis, m.	*fire*
*ignōrō, ignōrāre, ignōrāvī	*not know about, not know of*
*ignōscō, ignōscere, ignōvī + dat.	*forgive*
iī *see* eō	
*ille, illa, illud	*that, he, she*
hic ... ille	*this one ... that one, one man ... another man*
illīc	*there, in that place*

illūc	*there, to that place*
hūc ... illūc	*this way ... that way, one way ... another way*
illūcēscō, illūcēscere, illūxī	*dawn, grow bright*
imāgō, imāginis, f.	*image, picture, bust*
imber, imbris, m.	*rain*
immortālis, immortāle	*immortal*
*immōtus, immōta, immōtum	*still, motionless*
*impediō, impedīre, impedīvī, impedītus	*delay, hinder*
*imperātor, imperātōris, m.	*emperor*
*imperium, imperiī, n.	*empire, power, command*
*imperō, imperāre, imperāvī + dat.	*order, command*
impetrō, impetrāre, impetrāvī	*obtain*
implicō, implicāre, implicāvī, implicātus	*implicate, involve*
imprōvīsus, imprōvīsa, imprōvīsum	*unexpected, unforeseen*
*in + acc.	**(1)** *into, onto*
*in + abl.	**(2)** *in, on*
*inānis, ināne	*empty, meaningless*
*incēdō, incēdere, incessī	*march, stride*
*incendō, incendere, incendī, incēnsus	*burn, set on fire, set fire to*
incertus, incerta, incertum	*uncertain*
incīdō, incīdere, incīdī, incīsus	*cut open*
*incipiō, incipere, incēpī, inceptus	*begin*
incitō, incitāre, incitāvī, incitātus	*urge on, encourage*
inclūdō, inclūdere, inclūsī, inclūsus	*shut up*
*inde	*then*
indulgeō, indulgēre, indulsī + dat.	*give way to*
*īnfēlīx, gen. īnfēlīcis	*unlucky*
*īnferō, īnferre, intulī, inlātus	*bring in, bring on, bring against*
īnferus, īnfera, īnferum	*of the Underworld*
īnfestus, īnfesta, īnfestum	*hostile, dangerous*
ingenium, ingeniī, n.	*character*
*ingēns, gen. ingentis	*huge*
*ingredior, ingredī, ingressus sum	*enter*
inimīcus, inimīcī, m.	*enemy*
initium, initiī, n.	*beginning*
*iniūria, iniūriae, f.	*injustice, injury*
iniūstē	*unfairly*
inlātus *see* īnferō	
innocēns, gen. innocentis	*innocent*
innocentia, innocentiae, f.	*innocence*
inquiētus, inquiēta, inquiētum	*unsettled*
*inquit	*says, said*
īnsānus, īnsāna, īnsānum	*mad, crazy, insane*
īnscrībō, īnscrībere, īnscrīpsī, īnscrīptus	*write, inscribe*
*īnsidiae, īnsidiārum, f.pl.	*trap, ambush*

*īnspiciō, īnspicere, īnspexī,
   īnspectus   *look at, inspect, examine, search*
īnstō, īnstāre, īnstitī   *be pressing, threaten*
*īnstruō, īnstruere, īnstrūxī,
   īnstrūctus   *draw up, set up*
   sē īnstruere   *draw oneself up*
*īnsula, īnsulae, f.   *island; block of flats, apartment
                building*
īnsum, inesse, īnfuī   *be in, be inside*
*intellegō, intellegere,
   intellēxī, intellēctus *understand*
*intentē   *closely, carefully, intently*
*inter + *acc.*   *among, between*
   inter sē   *among themselves, with
                each other*
*intereā   *meanwhile*
*interficiō, interficere,
   interfēcī, interfectus *kill*
interpellō, interpellāre,
   interpellāvī   *interrupt*
interrogō, interrogāre,
   interrogāvī, interrogātus *question*
intrā + *acc.*   *inside*
intremō, intremere, intremuī *shake*
*intrō, intrāre, intrāvī   *enter*
*inveniō, invenīre, invēnī,
   inventus   *find*
invideō, invidēre, invīdī,
   invīsus   *envy, be jealous of*
*invidia, invidiae, f.   *jealousy, envy, unpopularity*
*invītō, invītāre, invītāvī,
   invītātus   *invite*
*invītus, invīta, invītum *unwilling, reluctant*
Iovis *see* Iuppiter
*ipse, ipsa, ipsum   *himself, herself, itself*
*īra, īrae, f.   *anger*
īrāscor, īrāscī, īrātus sum
   + *dat.*   *become angry with*
*īrātus, īrāta, īrātum   *angry*
īre *see* eō
*is, ea, id   *he, she, it, that*
   id quod   *what*
*iste, ista, istud   *that*
*ita   *in this way*
   sīcut ... ita   *just as ... so*
*ita vērō   *yes*
Ītalia, Ītaliae, f.   *Italy*
*itaque   *and so*
*iter, itineris, n.   *journey, progress*
*iterum   *again*
*iubeō, iubēre, iussī, iussus *order*
iūcundus, iūcunda,
   iūcundum   *pleasant*
*iūdex, iūdicis, m.   *judge*
*iungō, iungere, iūnxī, iūnctus *join*
Iūnō, Iūnōnis, f.   *Juno (goddess of marriage)*
Iuppiter, Iovis, m.   *Jupiter (god of the sky, greatest
              of Roman gods)*
iūrō, iūrāre, iūrāvī   *swear*
iussī *see* iubeō

*iussum, iussī, n.   *instruction, order*
   iussū Imperātōris   *at the Emperor's order*
*iuvenis, iuvenis, m.   *young man*
*iuvō, iuvāre, iūvī   *help, assist*

1

L. = Lūcius
*labor, labōris, m.   *work, labour*
*labōrō, labōrāre, labōrāvī *work*
*lacrima, lacrimae, f.   *tear*
*lacrimō, lacrimāre, lacrimāvī *weep, cry*
laetē   *happily*
*laetus, laeta, laetum   *happy*
langueō, languēre   *feel weak, feel ill*
lassō, lassāre, lassāvī,
   lassātus   *tire, weary*
*lateō, latēre, latuī   *lie hidden*
Latīnus, Latīna, Latīnum *Latin*
latrō, latrōnis, m.   *robber, thug*
lātus, lāta, lātum   *wide*
*laudō, laudāre, laudāvī,
   laudātus   *praise*
lectīca, lectīcae, f.   *litter, sedan-chair*
*lectus, lectī, m.   *couch, bed*
*lēgātus, lēgātī, m.   *commander*
lēgem *see* lēx
*legiō, legiōnis, f.   *legion*
*legō, legere, lēgī, lēctus *read*
lēniō, lēnīre, lēnīvī, lēnītus *soothe, calm down*
*lentē   *slowly*
*leō, leōnis, m.   *lion*
*levis, leve   *light, slight, trivial, changeable*
*lēx, lēgis, f.   *law*
libellus, libellī, m.   *little book*
*libenter   *gladly*
*liber, librī, m.   *book*
*līberālis, līberāle   *generous*
*līberī, līberōrum, m.pl. *children*
*līberō, līberāre, līberāvī,
   līberātus   *free, set free*
*lībertās, lībertātis, f.   *freedom*
*lībertus, lībertī, m.   *freedman, ex-slave*
librum *see* liber
*lībum, lībī, n.   *cake*
licet, licēre   *be allowed*
   mihi licet   *I am allowed*
*līmen, līminis, n.   *threshold, doorway*
lingua, linguae, f.   *tongue*
liquidus, liquida, liquidum *liquid*
līs, lītis, f.   *court case*
*littera, litterae, f.   *letter (of alphabet)*
*   litterae, litterārum, f.pl. *letter, letters
              (correspondence),
              literature*
*lītus, lītoris, n.   *sea-shore, shore*
*locus, locī, m.   *place*
longē   *far*

longē errāre	*make a big mistake*
longus, longa, longum	*long*
*loquor, loquī, locūtus sum	*speak*
lūcem *see* lūx	
*lūdus, lūdī, m.	*game*
*lūna, lūnae, f.	*moon*
lupus, lupī, m.	*wolf*
lūscus, lūsca, lūscum	*one-eyed*
*lūx, lūcis, f.	*light, daylight*

m

M. = Marcus	
M'. = Mānius	
madidus, madida, madidum	*soaked*
*magnopere	*greatly*
* magis	*more*
* maximē	*very greatly, very much, most of all*
*magnus, magna, magnum	*big, large, great*
maior, *gen.* maiōris	*bigger, larger, greater*
* maximus, maxima, maximum	*very big, very large, very great, greatest*
Pontifex Maximus	*Chief Priest*
*male	*badly, unfavourably*
malignus, maligna, malignum	*spiteful*
*mālō, mālle, māluī	*prefer*
*malus, mala, malum	*evil, bad*
peior, *gen.* peiōris	*worse*
* pessimus, pessima, pessimum	*worst, very bad*
*mandātum, mandātī, n.	*instruction, order*
*mandō, mandāre, mandāvī, mandātus	*order, entrust, hand over*
*māne	*in the morning*
*maneō, manēre, mānsī	*remain, stay*
in fidē manēre	*stay loyal*
*manus, manūs, f.	**(1)** *hand*
in manum convenīre	*pass into the hands of*
*manus, manūs, f.	**(2)** *band (of men)*
*mare, maris, n.	*sea*
*marītus, marītī, m.	*husband*
marmor, marmoris, n.	*marble*
Mārtiālis, Mārtiāle	*of Martial*
massa, massae, f.	*block*
*māter, mātris, f.	*mother*
mātrimōnium, mātrimōniī, n.	*marriage*
maximē *see* magnopere	
maximus *see* magnus	
mē *see* ego	
medicīna, medicīnae, f.	*medicine*
medicus, medicī, m.	*doctor*
meditor, meditārī, meditātus sum	*consider*
*medius, media, medium	*middle*
melior *see* bonus	

*mendāx, mendācis, m.	*liar*
mendāx, *gen.* mendācis	*lying, deceitful*
*mēnsa, mēnsae, f.	*table*
*mēnsis, mēnsis, m.	*month*
mentior, mentīrī, mentītus sum	*lie, tell a lie*
*mercātor, mercātōris, m.	*merchant*
mereō, merēre, meruī	*deserve*
mergō, mergere, mersī, mersus	*submerge*
metallum, metallī, n.	*a mine*
*metus, metūs, m.	*fear*
*meus, mea, meum	*my, mine*
mī Lupe	*my dear Lupus*
mihi *see* ego	
*mīles, mīlitis, m.	*soldier*
mīlitō, mīlitāre, mīlitāvī	*be a soldier*
*mīlle	*a thousand*
* mīlia	*thousands*
minae, minārum, f.pl.	*threats*
*minimē	*no, least, very little*
minimus *see* parvus	
minister, ministrī, m.	*servant, agent*
minor *see* parvus	
*minor, minārī, minātus sum + *dat.*	*threaten*
*mīrābilis, mīrābile	*extraordinary, strange, wonderful*
*mīror, mīrārī, mīrātus sum	*admire, wonder at*
mīrus, mīra, mīrum	*extraordinary*
*miser, misera, miserum	*miserable, wretched, sad*
Mithridāticum bellum	*the war with Mithridates*
*mittō, mittere, mīsī, missus	*send*
moderātiō, moderātiōnis, f.	*moderation, caution*
*modo	*just, now, only, just now*
nōn modo … sed etiam	*not only … but also*
*modus, modī, m.	*manner, way, kind*
* quō modō?	*how? in what way?*
moenia, moenium, n.pl.	*city walls*
molliō, mollīre, mollīvī, mollītus	*soothe*
*moneō, monēre, monuī, monitus	*warn, advise*
*mōns, montis, m.	*mountain*
mōns Palātīnus	*the Palatine hill*
summus mōns	*the top of the mountain*
*morbus, morbī, m.	*illness*
*morior, morī, mortuus sum	*die*
morere!	*die!*
* mortuus, mortua, mortuum	*dead*
*moror, morārī, morātus sum	*delay*
*mors, mortis, f.	*death*
mortem sibi cōnscīscere	*commit suicide*
mortālis, mortāle	*mortal*
genus mortāle	*the human race*
mortuus *see* morior	
mōs, mōris, m.	*custom*
mōtus, mōtūs, m.	*movement*
*moveō, movēre, mōvī, mōtus	*move, influence*

*mox	soon	*nimis	too
multitūdō, multitūdinis, f.	crowd	*nimium	too much
*multus, multa, multum	much	*nisi	except, unless
* multī, multae, multa	many	niveus, nivea, niveum	snow-white
* multō	much	nō, nāre, nāvī	swim
* plūrimī, plūrimae,		*nōbilis, nōbile	noble, of noble birth
plūrima	very many	nōbīs see nōs	
* plūrimus, plūrima,		*noceō, nocēre, nocuī + dat.	hurt, harm
plūrimum	most	nocte see nox	
* plūs, gen. plūris	more	*nōlō, nōlle, nōluī	not want
quid multa?	what more is there to say?, in short	nōlī, nōlīte	do not, don't
		*nōmen, nōminis, n.	name
mūniō, mūnīre, mūnīvī,		nōminō, nōmināre, nōmināvī,	
mūnītus	protect, immunise	nōminātus	name, mention by name
*mūrus, mūrī, m.	wall	*nōn	not
musca, muscae, f.	fly	*nōnāgintā	ninety
mūsicus, mūsicī, m.	musician	*nōnne?	surely?
mūtābilis, mūtābile	changeable, contradictory	*nōnnūllī, nōnnūllae,	
*mūtō, mūtāre, mūtāvī,		nōnnūlla	some, several
mūtātus	change	nōnnumquam	sometimes
vestem mūtāre	put on mourning clothes	nōnus, nōna, nōnum	ninth
		*nōs	we, us
		*noster, nostra, nostrum	our
		*nōtus, nōta, nōtum	known, well-known, famous
		Notus, Notī, m.	South wind

—————— **n** ——————

		*novem	nine
		*nōvī	I know
*nam	for	*novus, nova, novum	new
nārrātiō, nārrātiōnis, f.	narration	*nox, noctis, f.	night
*nārrō, nārrāre, nārrāvī,		*nūbō, nūbere, nūpsī + dat.	marry
nārrātus	tell, relate	nūgae, nūgārum, f.pl.	nonsense, foolish talk
*nāscor, nāscī, nātus sum	be born	*nūllus, nūlla, nūllum	not any, no
* nātus, nāta, nātum	born	*num?	(1) surely … not?
septuāgintā annōs nātus	seventy years old	*num	(2) whether
nat see nō		*numerus, numerī, m.	number
natō, natāre, natāvī	swim	*numquam	never
nātus see nāscor		*nunc	now
*nauta, nautae, m.	sailor	*nūntiō, nūntiāre, nūntiāvī,	
*nāvigō, nāvigāre, nāvigāvī	sail	nūntiātus	announce
*nāvis, nāvis, f.	ship	*nūntius, nūntiī, m.	messenger, news
*nē	that … not, so that … not, in order that … not	*nūper	recently
		nūpsī see nūbō	
* nē … quidem	not even	nūptiae, nūptiārum, f.pl.	wedding, marriage
*nec	and not, nor	nūptiālis, nūptiāle	wedding, marriage
* nec … nec	neither … nor	tabulae nūptiālēs	marriage contract, marriage tablets
*necesse	necessary		
*necō, necāre, necāvī,		nūptūrus see nūbō	
necātus	kill	*nusquam	nowhere
*neglegō, neglegere, neglēxī,			
neglēctus	neglect, ignore, disregard		
*negōtium, negōtiī, n.	business		
*nēmō	no one, nobody		
Neptūnus, Neptūnī, m.	Neptune (god of the sea)		
neque	and not, nor	—————— **o** ——————	
* neque … neque	neither … nor		
*nescio, nescīre, nescīvī	not know		
*niger, nigra, nigrum	black	*obiciō, obicere, obiēcī,	
*nihil	nothing	obiectus	present, put in the way of, expose to
nihil cūrō	I don't care	*oblīvīscor, oblīvīscī, oblītus	
nihilōminus	nevertheless	sum	forget
nimbus, nimbī, m.	rain-cloud	obscūrus, obscūra, obscūrum	dark, gloomy

*obstō, obstāre, obstitī + *dat.*	obstruct, block the way
obstupefaciō, obstupefacere, obstupefēcī, obstupefactus	amaze, stun
obtineō, obtinēre, obtinuī, obtentus	hold
obtulī *see* offerō	
occāsiō, occāsiōnis, f.	opportunity
*occīdō, occīdere, occīdī, occīsus	kill
occidō, occidere, occidī	set
occupātus, occupāta, occupātum	busy
occupō, occupāre, occupāvī, occupātus	seize, take over
octāvus, octāva, octāvum	eighth
*octō	eight
*octōgintā	eighty
*oculus, oculī, m.	eye
*ōdī	I hate
odiōsus, odiōsa, odiōsum	hateful
*odium, odiī, n.	hatred
odiō esse	be hateful
offendō, offendere, offendī, offēnsus	displease, offend
*offerō, offerre, obtulī, oblātus	offer
officium, officiī, n.	duty
*ōlim	once, some time ago
ōmen, ōminis, n.	omen (sign from the gods)
*omnīnō	completely
*omnis, omne	all
omnia	all, everything
*opēs, opum, f.pl.	money, wealth
*oppidum, oppidī, n.	town
*opprimō, opprimere, oppressī, oppressus	crush
*oppugnō, oppugnāre, oppugnāvī, oppugnātus	attack
optimē *see* bene	
optimus *see* bonus	
*opus, operis, n.	work, construction
orbis, orbis, m.	globe, world
ōrdō, ōrdinis, m.	row, line
*orior, orīrī, ortus sum	rise, arise
*ōrnō, ōrnāre, ōrnāvī, ōrnātus	decorate
ōrnātus, ōrnāta, ōrnātum	decorated, elaborately furnished
*ōrō, ōrāre, ōrāvī	beg
*ostendō, ostendere, ostendī, ostentus	show
*ōtiōsus, ōtiōsa, ōtiōsum	idle, on holiday
ōtium, ōtiī, n.	leisure
Ovidiānus, Ovidiāna, Ovidiānum	of Ovid
ovis, ovis, f.	sheep

p

pācem *see* pāx	
*paene	nearly, almost
Palātīnus, Palātīna, Palātīnum	Palatine
mōns Palātīnus	the Palatine hill
pallēscō, pallēscere, palluī	grow pale
pantomīmus, pantomīmī, m.	pantomimus, dancer
pār, *gen.* paris	equal
*parcō, parcere, pepercī + *dat.*	spare
parēns, parentis, m.f.	parent
*pāreō, pārēre, pāruī	obey
*parō, parāre, parāvī, parātus	prepare
parātus, parāta, parātum	ready, prepared
*pars, partis, f.	part
*parvus, parva, parvum	small, little
minor, *gen.* minōris	less, smaller
* minimus, minima, minimum	very little, least
passus *see* patior	
*patefaciō, patefacere, patefēcī, patefactus	reveal
*pater, patris, m.	father
*patior, patī, passus sum	suffer, endure
*patria, patriae, f.	country, homeland
patrōnus, patrōnī, m.	patron
*paucī, paucae, pauca	few, a few
paulīsper	for a short time
*paulō	a little
*pauper, *gen.* pauperis	poor
paveō, pavēre, pāvī	dread, fear
*pavor, pavōris, m.	panic
*pāx, pācis, f.	peace
*pecūnia, pecūniae, f.	money
pedem *see* pēs	
peior *see* malus	
*per + *acc.*	through, along
percutiō, percutere, percussī, percussus	strike
*pereō, perīre, periī	die, perish
*perficiō, perficere, perfēcī, perfectus	finish
perīculōsus, perīculōsa, perīculōsum	dangerous
perīculum, perīculī, n.	danger
periī *see* pereō	
*perītus, perīta, perītum	skilful
periūrium, periūriī, n.	false oath, perjury
*persuādeō, persuādēre, persuāsī + *dat.*	persuade
*perterreō, perterrēre, perterruī, perterritus	terrify
*perturbō, perturbāre, perturbāvī, perturbātus	disturb, alarm
*perveniō, pervenīre, pervēnī	reach, arrive at
*pēs, pedis, m.	foot, paw
pessimus *see* malus	

*petō, petere, petīvī, petītus — make for, attack; seek, beg for, ask for
phōca, phōcae, f. — seal
pietās, pietātis, f. — duty
piscis, piscis, m. — fish
*placeō, placēre, placuī + dat. — please, suit
*plaudō, plaudere, plausī, plausus — applaud, clap
plausus, plausūs, m. — applause
*plēnus, plēna, plēnum — full
plūrēs, plūrimī see multus
*poena, poenae, f. — punishment
*   poenās dare — pay the penalty, be punished
*poēta, poētae, m. — poet
*polliceor, pollicērī, pollicitus sum — promise
pompa, pompae, f. — procession
*pōnō, pōnere, posuī, positus — place, put, put up
*pōns, pontis, m. — bridge
pontifex, pontificis, m. — priest
     Pontifex Maximus — Chief Priest
pontus, pontī, m. — sea
poposcī see poscō
*populus, populī, m. — people
*porta, portae, f. — gate
*portō, portāre, portāvī, portātus — carry
*portus, portūs, m. — harbour
*poscō, poscere, poposcī — demand, ask for
possideō, possidēre, possēdī, possessus — possess
*possum, posse, potuī — can, be able
*post + acc. — after, behind
*posteā — afterwards
*postquam — after, when
postrēmō — finally, lastly
*postrīdiē — on the next day
*postulō, postulāre, postulāvī, postulātus — demand
pote see quis
potēns, gen. potentis — powerful
potēs see possum
*potestās, potestātis, f. — power, control
     in potestātem redigere — bring under the control
*praebeō, praebēre, praebuī, praebitus — offer, provide
*praeceps, gen. praecipitis — headlong
praecipitō, praecipitāre, praecipitāvī — hurl
     sē praecipitāre — hurl oneself
praecō, praecōnis, m. — herald, announcer
praeficiō, praeficere, praefēcī, praefectus — put in charge
*praemium, praemiī, n. — prize, reward, profit
*praesertim — especially
praesum, praeesse, praefuī + dat. — be in charge of
*praeter + acc. — except
praetereā — besides

praetōriānus, praetōriāna, praetōriānum — praetorian (belonging to emperor's bodyguard)
precēs, precum, f.pl. — prayers
*precor, precārī, precātus sum — pray (to)
pretiōsus, pretiōsa, pretiōsum — expensive, precious
*pretium, pretiī, n. — price
prīdiē — the day before
prīmum — first
     cum prīmum — as soon as
*prīmus, prīma, prīmum — first
*prīnceps, prīncipis, m. — chief, chieftain, emperor
prīncipātus, prīncipātūs, m. — principate, reign
prior — first, in front, earlier
*prius — earlier
*priusquam — before, until
prīvātus, prīvāta, prīvātum — private
*prō + abl. — in front of, for, in return for
*   prō certō habēre — know for certain
*probō, probāre, probāvī — prove
*prōcēdō, prōcēdere, prōcessī — advance, proceed
*procul — far off
*prōdō, prōdere, prōdidī, prōditus — betray
*proelium, proeliī, n. — battle
*proficīscor, proficīscī, profectus sum — set out
*prōgredior, prōgredī, prōgressus sum — advance
*prohibeō, prohibēre, prohibuī, prohibitus — prevent
*prōmittō, prōmittere, prōmīsī, prōmissus — promise
prōnūntiō, prōnūntiāre, prōnūntiāvī, prōnūntiātus — proclaim, preach, announce
*prope + acc. — near
properō, properāre, properāvī — hurry
prōpōnō, prōpōnere, prōposuī, prōpositus — propose, put forward
prōsiliō, prōsilīre, prōsiluī — leap forward, jump
prōtinus — immediately
prōvincia, prōvinciae, f. — province
*proximus, proxima, proximum — nearest, next to, last
prūdenter — prudently, sensibly
pūblicō, pūblicāre, pūblicāvī, pūblicātus — confiscate
pūblicus, pūblica, pūblicum — public
*puella, puellae, f. — girl
*puer, puerī, m. — boy
pugiō, pugiōnis, m. — dagger
*pugna, pugnae, f. — fight
*pugnō, pugnāre, pugnāvī — fight
*pulcher, pulchra, pulchrum — beautiful
*pulsō, pulsāre, pulsāvī, pulsātus — hit, knock at, thump, punch
pūmiliō, pūmiliōnis, m. — dwarf
Pūnicus, Pūnica, Pūnicum — Carthaginian, Punic
*pūniō, pūnīre, pūnīvī, pūnītus — punish
*puto, putāre, putāvī — think

q

Q. = Quīntus
quā — *where*
*quadrāgintā — *forty*
quadrīga, quadrīgae, f. — *chariot*
*quaerō, quaerere, quaesīvī, quaesītus — *search for, look for*
quaesō — *I beg, i.e. please*
*quālis, quāle — *what sort of*
*quam — **(1)** *how*
    quam celerrimē — *as quickly as possible*
*quam — **(2)** *than*
*quamquam — *although*
*quandō? — *when?*
*quantus, quanta, quantum — *how big*
*quārē? — *why?*
quārtus, quārta, quārtum — *fourth*
*quasi — *as if*
*quattuor — *four*
quattuordecim — *fourteen*
*-que — *and*
    -que … -que — *both … and*
quendam *see* quīdam
querēla, querēlae, f. — *complaint*
*queror, querī, questus sum — *lament, complain about*
*quī, quae, quod — *who, which*
    id quod — *what*
    quod sī — *but if*
quī? quae? quod? — *which? what?*
*quia — *because*
*quicquam (*also spelt* quidquam) — *anything*
quicquid — *whatever*
quīcumque, quaecumque, quodcumque — *whoever, whatever, any whatever*
quid? *see* quis?
*quīdam, quaedam, quoddam — *one, a certain*
*quidem — *indeed*
* nē … quidem — *not even*
quiēs, quiētis, f. — *rest*
quīndecim — *fifteen*
*quīnquāgintā — *fifty*
*quīnque — *five*
quīntus, quīnta, quīntum — *fifth*
*quis? quid? — *who? what?*
    quid agis? — *how are you? how are you getting on?*
    quid faciam? — *what am I to do?*
    quid multa? — *what more is there to say?, in short*
    quid pote? — *what could be?*
*quō? — *where? where to?*
*quō modō? — *how? in what way?*
*quod — *because*
    ideō quod — *for the reason that, because*
    quod sī — *but if*

quōdam *see* quīdam
*quondam — *one day, once*
*quoque — *also, too*
quōsdam *see* quīdam
*quot? — *how many?*
*quotiēns — *whenever*

r

*rapiō, rapere, rapuī, raptus — *seize, grab*
rārō — *rarely*
ratiō, ratiōnis, f. — *reason*
rē *see* rēs
rebellō, rebellāre, rebellāvī — *rebel, revolt*
rēbus *see* rēs
*recipiō, recipere, recēpī, receptus — *recover, take back*
recitātiō, recitātiōnis, f. — *recital, public reading*
*recitō, recitāre, recitāvī, recitātus — *recite, read out*
rēctē — *rightly*
*recūsō, recūsāre, recūsāvī, recūsātus — *refuse*
*reddō, reddere, reddidī, redditus — *give back, make*
*redeō, redīre, rediī — *return, go back, come back*
redigō, redigere, redēgī, redāctus — *bring*
    in potestātem redigere — *bring under the control*
*referō, referre, rettulī, relātus — *bring back, carry, deliver, tell, report*
    victōriam referre — *win a victory*
*reficiō, reficere, refēcī, refectus — *repair*
*rēgīna, rēgīnae, f. — *queen*
regiō, regiōnis, f. — *region*
rēgis *see* rēx
*rēgnum, rēgnī, n. — *kingdom*
*regō, regere, rēxī, rēctus — *rule*
*regredior, regredī, regressus sum — *go back, return*
relēgō, relēgāre, relēgāvī, relēgātus — *exile*
*relinquō, relinquere, relīquī, relictus — *leave*
reliquiae, reliquiārum, f.pl. — *remains*
rem *see* rēs
rēmigō, rēmigāre, rēmigāvī — *row*
rēmus, rēmī, m. — *oar*
renovō, renovāre, renovāvī, renovātus — *renew, resume, continue*
repente — *suddenly*
reprehendō, reprehendere, reprehendī, reprehēnsus — *blame, criticise*
repudiō, repudiāre, repudiāvī, repudiātus — *divorce*
*rēs, reī, f. — *thing, business*
* rē vērā — *in fact, truly, really*

rem cōgitāre	*consider the problem*	*sapiēns, *gen.* sapientis	*wise*
rem nārrāre	*tell the story*	*satis	*enough*
* rēs adversae	*misfortune*	*saxum, saxī, n.	*rock*
*resistō, resistere, restitī + *dat.*	*resist*	scaena, scaenae, f.	*stage, scene*
respiciō, respicere, respexī	*look at, look upon, look up*	extrēma scaena	*the edge of the stage*
*respondeō, respondēre,		scelerātus, scelerāta,	
respondī	*reply*	scelerātum	*wicked*
respōnsum, respōnsī, n.	*answer*	*scelestus, scelesta, scelestum	*wicked*
restituō, restituere, restituī,		*scelus, sceleris, n.	*crime*
restitūtus	*restore*	scīlicet	*obviously*
resūmō, resūmere, resūmpsī,		*scindō, scindere, scidī,	
resūmptus	*pick up again*	scissus	*tear, tear up, cut up*
retineō, retinēre, retinuī,		*scio, scīre, scīvī	*know*
retentus	*keep, hold back*	*scrībō, scrībere, scrīpsī,	
rettulī *see* referō		scrīptus	*write*
*reveniō, revenīre, revēnī	*come back, return*	sculptor, sculptōris, m.	*sculptor*
revertor, revertī, reversus		scurrīlis, scurrīle	*rude, impudent*
sum	*turn back, return*	*sē	*himself, herself, themselves*
*revocō, revocāre, revocāvī,		inter sē	*among themselves,*
revocātus	*recall, call back*		*with each other*
*rēx, rēgis, m.	*king*	*secō, secāre, secuī, sectus	*cut, carve*
rhētor, rhētoris, m.	*teacher*	sēcrētus, sēcrēta, sēcrētum	*secret*
*rīdeō, rīdēre, rīsī	*laugh, smile*	secundus, secunda,	
rīdiculus, rīdicula, rīdiculum	*ridiculous, silly*	secundum	*second*
rīpa, rīpae, f.	*river bank*	secūris, secūris, f.	*axe*
rīsus, rīsūs, m.	*smile*	*sēcūrus, sēcūra, sēcūrum	*without a care*
*rogō, rogāre, rogāvī, rogātus	*ask*	*sed	*but*
Rōma, Rōmae, f.	*Rome*	sēdecim	*sixteen*
Rōmae	*at Rome*	*sedeō, sedēre, sēdī	*sit*
Rōmānī, Rōmānōrum, m.pl.	*Romans*	sēdō, sēdāre, sēdāvī, sēdātus	*quell, calm down*
Rōmānus, Rōmāna,		seges, segetis, f.	*crop, harvest*
Rōmānum	*Roman*	sēiūnctus, sēiūncta,	
ruīna, ruīnae, f.	*ruin, wreckage*	sēiūnctum	*separate*
*ruō, ruere, ruī	*rush*	sella, sellae, f.	*chair*
*rūrsus	*again*	*semper	*always*
*rūs, rūris, n.	*country, countryside*	*senātor, senātōris, m.	*senator*
rūsticus, rūstica, rūsticum	*country, in the country*	senātus, senātūs, m.	*senate*
vīlla rūstica	*house in the country*	cognitiō senātūs	*trial by the senate*
		*senex, senis, m.	*old man*
		sēnsus, sēnsūs, m.	*feeling*
		*sententia, sententiae, f.	*opinion, sentence*
———— S ————		*sentiō, sentīre, sēnsī, sēnsus	*feel, notice*
		*septem	*seven*
		septendecim	*seventeen*
		septimus, septima, septimum	*seventh*
*sacer, sacra, sacrum	*sacred*	*septuāgintā	*seventy*
*sacerdōs, sacerdōtis, m.f.	*priest*	*sequor, sequī, secūtus sum	*follow*
sacerdōtium, sacerdōtiī, n.	*priesthood*	serēnus, serēna, serēnum	*calm, clear*
sacrificium, sacrificiī, n.	*offering, sacrifice*	sermō, sermōnis, m.	*conversation*
sacrificō, sacrificāre,		*servō, servāre, servāvī,	
sacrificāvī, sacrificātus	*sacrifice*	servātus	*save, look after, preserve*
*saepe	*often*	*servus, servī, m.	*slave*
*saevus, saeva, saevum	*savage, cruel*	*sex	*six*
saltātrīx, saltātrīcis, f.	*dancing-girl*	*sexāgintā	*sixty*
*salūs, salūtis, f.	*safety, health*	sextus, sexta, sextum	*sixth*
salūtem dīcere	*send good wishes*	*sī	*if*
*salūtō, salūtāre, salūtāvī,		quod sī	*but if*
salūtātus	*greet*	sibi *see* sē	
*salvē! salvēte!	*hello!*	*sīc	*thus, in this way*
*sanguis, sanguinis, m.	*blood*	*sīcut	*like*
sānō, sānāre, sānāvī, sānātus	*heal, cure*		

sīcut … ita	just as … so
sīdus, sīderis, n.	star
significō, significāre, significāvī, significātus	mean, indicate
signō, signāre, signāvī, signātus	sign, seal
*signum, signī, n.	sign, seal, signal
silentium, silentiī, n.	silence
*silva, silvae, f.	wood
sim see sum	
*similis, simile	similar
simplex, gen. simplicis	simple
*simul	at the same time
*simulac, simulatque	as soon as
*simulō, simulāre, simulāvī, simulātus	pretend
*sine + abl.	without
sistō, sistere, stitī	stop, halt
socia, sociae, f.	companion, partner
*socius, sociī, m.	companion, partner
*sōl, sōlis, m.	sun
*soleō, solēre	be accustomed
sollemnis, sollemne	solemn, traditional
sollemniter	solemnly
sollicitō, sollicitāre, sollicitāvī, sollicitātus	worry
*sollicitus, sollicita, sollicitum	worried, anxious
*sōlus, sōla, sōlum	alone, lonely, only, on one's own
somnus, somnī, m.	sleep
*sonitus, sonitūs, m.	sound
sonō, sonāre, sonuī	sound, sound off
*soror, sorōris, f.	sister
spē see spēs	
speciēs, speciēī, f.	appearance
*spectāculum, spectāculī, n.	show, spectacle
spectātor, spectātōris, m.	spectator
*spectō, spectāre, spectāvī, spectātus	look at, watch
*spernō, spernere, sprēvī, sprētus	despise, reject, ignore
*spērō, spērāre, spērāvī	hope, expect
*spēs, speī, f.	hope
splendidus, splendida, splendidum	splendid, impressive
sportula, sportulae, f.	handout
st!	hush!
stābam see stō	
*statim	at once
statua, statuae, f.	statue
*stilus, stilī, m.	pen (pointed stick for writing on wax tablet)
*stō, stāre, stetī	stand, lie at anchor
strēnuē	hard, energetically
strepitus, strepitūs, m.	noise, din
*studium, studiī, n.	enthusiasm, keenness; study
*stultus, stulta, stultum	stupid, foolish
*suādeō, suādēre, suāsī + dat.	advise, suggest
*suāvis, suāve	sweet
suāviter	sweetly
*sub + abl.	under, beneath
*subitō	suddenly
*subveniō, subvenīre, subvēnī + dat.	help, come to help
*sum, esse, fuī	be
*summus, summa, summum	highest, greatest, top
summus mōns	the top of the mountain
sūmptuōsus, sūmptuōsa, sūmptuōsum	expensive, lavish, costly
superbē	arrogantly
*superbus, superba, superbum	arrogant, proud
supercilia, superciliōrum, n.pl.	eyebrows
supercilia contrahere	draw eyebrows together, frown
*superō, superāre, superāvī, superātus	overcome, overpower
superpōnō, superpōnere, superposuī, superpositus	place on
superstes, superstitis, m.	survivor
suppliciter	like a suppliant, humbly
supprimō, supprimere, suppressī, suppressus	staunch, stop flow of
suprā + acc.	over, on top of
*surgō, surgere, surrēxī	get up, rise
suscipiō, suscipere, suscēpī, susceptus	undertake, take on
suspīciō, suspīciōnis, f.	suspicion
*suspicor, suspicārī, suspicātus sum	suspect
sustulī see tollere	
susurrō, susurrāre, susurrāvī	whisper, mutter
*suus, sua, suum	his, her, their, his own, their own

——————— t ———————

T. = Titus	
*taberna, tabernae, f.	shop, inn
tablīnum, tablīnī, n.	study
tabula, tabulae, f.	tablet, writing-tablet
tabulae nūptiālēs	marriage contract, marriage tablets
*taceō, tacēre, tacuī	be silent, be quiet
tacē!	shut up! be quiet!
*tacitē	quietly, silently
*tacitus, tacita, tacitum	quiet, silent, in silence
*tālis, tāle	such
*tam	so
*tamen	however
tamquam	as, like
*tandem	at last
*tangō, tangere, tetigī, tāctus	touch
tantum	only
*tantus, tanta, tantum	so great, such a great
tantī esse	be worth
taurus, taurī, m.	bull
tē see tū	

tēctum, tēctī, n.	ceiling, roof
tellūs, tellūris, f.	land, earth
*tempestās, tempestātis, f.	storm
*templum, templī, n.	temple
*temptō, temptāre, temptāvī, temptātus	try, put to the test
*tempus, temporis, n.	time
*teneō, tenēre, tenuī, tentus	hold
*terra, terrae, f.	ground, land
*terreō, terrēre, terruī, territus	frighten
tertius, tertia, tertium	third
testāmentum, testāmentī, n.	will
testimōnium, testimōniī, n.	evidence
*testis, testis, m.f.	witness
testor, testārī, testātus sum	call to witness
tetigī see tangere	
theātrum, theātrī, n.	theatre
thermae, thermārum, f.pl.	baths
Ti. = Tiberius	
Tiberis, Tiberis, m.	river Tiber
tibi see tū	
tībia, tībiae, f.	pipe
tībiīs cantāre	play on the pipes
*timeō, timēre, timuī	be afraid, fear
timidē	nervously, fearfully
timidus, timida, timidum	fearful, frightened
*timor, timōris, m.	fear
toga, togae, f.	toga
*tollō, tollere, sustulī, sublātus	raise, lift up, hold up; remove, do away with
torus, torī, m.	bed
*tot	so many
*tōtus, tōta, tōtum	whole
*trādō, trādere, trādidī, trāditus	hand over
*trahō, trahere, trāxī, tractus	drag
*trāns + acc.	across
*trānseō, trānsīre, trānsiī	cross
trānsfīgō, trānsfigere, trānsfīxī, trānsfīxus	pierce, stab
trēdecim	thirteen
tremō, tremere, tremuī	tremble, shake
*trēs, tria	three
tribūnus, tribūnī, m.	tribune (high-ranking officer)
triclīnium, triclīniī, n.	dining-room
tridēns, tridentis, m.	trident
*trīgintā	thirty
*trīstis, trīste	sad
triumphus, triumphī, m.	triumph
triumphum agere	celebrate a triumph
*tū, tuī	you (singular)
tulī see ferō	
*tum	then
tum dēmum	then at last, only then
tumultus, tumultūs, m.	riot
tumulus, tumulī, m.	tomb
*turba, turbae, f.	crowd
turpis, turpe	shameful
*tūtus, tūta, tūtum	safe

*tuus, tua, tuum	your (singular), yours
tyrannus, tyrannī, m.	tyrant

u

*ubi	where, when
*ubīque	everywhere
*ūllus, ūlla, ūllum	any
ulmus, ulmī, f.	elm tree
*ultimus, ultima, ultimum	furthest, last
ultiō, ultiōnis, f.	revenge
umbra, umbrae, f.	shadow, ghost
*umquam	ever
*unda, undae, f.	wave
*unde	from where
*undique	on all sides, from all sides
*ūnus, ūna, ūnum	one
*urbs, urbis, f.	city
ūsus, ūsūs, m.	use
ūsuī esse	be of use
*ut	(1) as
*ut	(2) that, so that, in order that
uterque, utraque, utrumque	each, both
*ūtor, ūtī, ūsus sum	use
*utrum	whether
* utrum … an	whether … or
*uxor, uxōris, f.	wife
uxōrem dūcere	take as a wife, marry

v

vagus, vaga, vagum	wandering
*valdē	very much, very
*valē	goodbye, farewell
valedīcō, valedīcēre, valedīxī	say goodbye
*validus, valida, validum	strong
*vehementer	violently, loudly
*vehō, vehere, vexī, vectus	carry
*vel	or
velim see volō	
vēna, vēnae, f.	vein
*vēndō, vēndere, vēndidī, vēnditus	sell
*venēnum, venēnī, n.	poison
venia, veniae, f.	mercy
*veniō, venīre, vēnī	come
vēnor, vēnārī, vēnātus sum	hunt
*ventus, ventī, m.	wind
*verberō, verberāre, verberāvī, verberātus	strike, beat
*verbum, verbī, n.	word
*vereor, verērī, veritus sum	be afraid, fear
*vērō	indeed
versus, versūs, m.	verse, line of poetry

vertex, verticis, m.	top, peak	*vīnum, vīnī, n.	wine
*vertō, vertere, vertī, versus	turn	*vir, virī, m.	man, husband
sē vertere	turn round	*virgō, virginis, f.	virgin
vertor, vertī, versus sum	turn	*virtūs, virtūtis, f.	courage, virtue
*vērum, vērī, n.	truth, the truth	vīs, f.	force, violence
*vērus, vēra, vērum	true, real	vīs see volō	
* rē vērā	in fact, truly, really	vīsitō, vīsitāre, vīsitāvī,	
vespillō, vespillōnis, m.	undertaker	vīsitātus	visit
*vester, vestra, vestrum	your (plural)	vīsus see videō	
*vestīmenta, vestīmentōrum,		*vīta, vītae, f.	life
n.pl.	clothes	*vītō, vītāre, vītāvī, vītātus	avoid
vestis, vestis, f.	clothing, clothes	*vituperō, vituperāre,	
vestem mūtāre	put on mourning clothes	vituperāvī, vituperātus	blame, curse
*vetus, gen. veteris	old	*vīvō, vīvere, vīxī	live, be alive
*vexō, vexāre, vexāvī, vexātus	annoy	*vīvus, vīva, vīvum	alive, living
vī see vīs		*vix	hardly, scarcely, with
*via, viae, f.	street, way		difficulty
Via Sacra, Viae Sacrae, f.	the Sacred Way (road		
	running through the	vōbīs see vōs	
	Forum)	vōcem see vōx	
vīcīnus, vīcīnī, m.	neighbour	*vocō, vocāre, vocāvī, vocātus	call
victima, victimae, f.	victim	*volō, velle, voluī	want
victor, victōris, m.	victor, winner	velim	I should like
victōria, victōriae, f.	victory	volucris, volucris, f.	bird
victōriam referre	win a victory	*volvō, volvere, volvī, volūtus	turn, roll
victus see vincō		in animō volvere	wonder, turn over in
*videō, vidēre, vīdī, vīsus	see		the mind
*videor, vidērī, vīsus sum	seem	*vōs	you (plural)
*vīgintī	twenty	vōbīscum	with you (plural)
vīlis, vīle	cheap	*vōx, vōcis, f.	voice
vīlla, vīllae, f.	house, villa	*vulnerō, vulnerāre, vulnerāvī,	
*vinciō, vincīre, vīnxī, vīnctus	bind, tie up	vulnerātus	wound, injure
*vincō, vincere, vīcī, victus	conquer, win, be victorious	*vulnus, vulneris, n.	wound
vindicō, vindicāre, vindicāvī,		vult see volō	
vindicātus	avenge	*vultus, vultūs, m.	expression, face